Running Your Own
ESTATE AGENCY

Running Your Own
ESTATE AGENCY

Val Redding

Kogan Page
WORKING
for
YOURSELF
Series

Front cover photograph courtesy of
Rolfe East & Co, Estate Agents, London W5

Copyright © Val Redding 1988

All rights reserved. No reproduction, copy or transmission of this publication may be made without written permission.

No paragraph of this publication may be reproduced, copied or transmitted save with written permission or in accordance with the provisions of the Copyright Act 1956 (as amended), or under the terms of any licence permitting limited copying issued by the Copyright Licensing Agency, 7 Ridgmount Street, London WC1E 7AE.

Any person who does any unauthorised act in relation to this publication may be liable to criminal prosecution and civil claims for damages.

First published in Great Britain in 1988 by Kogan Page Limited, 120 Pentonville Road, London N1 9JN

British Library Cataloguing in Publication Data

Redding, Val
   Running your own estate agency.—(Kogan Page working for yourself series).
   1. England. Estate agency – Manuals
   I. Title
   333.33'0942

ISBN 1-85091-620-9

Printed and bound in Great Britain by
Biddles Ltd, Guildford

Contents

Preface   7

1. Starting the Business   9

    Introduction 9; Sole trader 9; The limited company 10; Partnerships 11; Raising the finance 12; Buying an existing agency 14; Choosing the right premises 15; Health and Safety at Work Act 1974 17; Planning permission 17; Insurance 18; Offering mortgage facilities 18; Surveying services 20; Employing staff 20; Value Added Tax 24; What makes a profit? 24; Keeping the books 25; Your business name 27; The importance of image 27; The importance of first contact 32; Business growth by recommendation 33; Efficient record keeping 33; Why should customers choose you? 37; Conclusion 38; Assignment 1: Assessing the competition 39

2. The Art of Good Salesmanship   41

    Introduction 41; Identifying your customer's needs 41; Every enquiry is potential business 43; Providing information 44; The personal touch 45; Making viewing arrangements 46; Making the sale 48; The right buyer for the right house 48; Contract races 51; Putting forward offers 51; Confirming the details 52; Dealing with fixtures and fittings 54; Handling deposits 55; Making sure completion is reached 55; Conclusion 58; Assignment 2: Viewing analysis 58; Assignment 3: Problem solving 59

3. Building Up Your Register   61

    Introduction 61; Getting off the ground 61; Turning enquiries into instructions 62; Touting – the dangers 63; Valuations 63; Putting the property to auction 67; Clinching the instruction 68; Confirming a valuation 70; Preparing specifications 70; Presenting specifications 72; Confirming the instruction in writing 74; Changing market conditions 75; Leasehold properties 76; On-site sales 77; National House Building Council 78; Selling on behalf of executors 78;

Property with part possession 79; Selling ex-council houses 79; Conclusion 80; Assignment 4: Securing instructions to sell 80; Assignment 5: Presentation of specifications 81

4. Your Role as Financial Adviser — 82

Introduction 82; Arranging mortgages 83; Understanding mortgages 85; Tax relief 90; Interest rates 91; The term of the advance 91; Understanding the constraints 91; Mortgage guarantee policy 92; Insurances 92; The right advice for your customer 94; What other expenses will your customer face? 95; Receiving inspection fees and checking mortgage application forms 99; Legal expenses 102; DIY conveyancing 105; Bridging finance 105; Budget plans for your customers 105; Accounting for deposits 108; Conclusion 108; Assignment 6: Understanding mortgages 109; Assignment 7: Preparing a budget plan 109

5. The Final Points — 111

Introduction 111; What is a conveyance? 112; National Association of Estate Agents 117; Further professional qualifications 118; Success breeds growth 121; Selling property in Scotland 123; Lettings 124; Glossary of legal terms 125; Conclusion 128; Assignment 8: Final project 128

Appendix: Sources of further information — 133

Further Reading from Kogan Page — 139

Index — 140

Preface

Starting any new business is an exciting if nerve-racking experience, but over the past few years many people who have been made redundant, or who have just felt the need to branch out on their own, have taken up the challenge. From this a whole new era of enterprise has been born, bringing with it a range of new businesses with new skills and new ideas which continue to flourish and grow.

Estate agency, however, is not a new concept, and whatever your reason is for choosing this field, you must remember that moving house touches upon one of our most basic needs – that of building a 'nest' for ourselves and our family. The role of the estate agent is therefore a very special one indeed.

The property market today is a complex and ever-changing one – a world influenced by the state of the economy, the building industry, even by the season of the year. It is exciting and demanding and can provide a challenging and very rewarding career for those who are successful in it. But gone are the days when agents simply take the measurements of a property, send a prospective buyer to view, negotiate a price and then write a few letters to confirm the deal. If you think this is all agency work consists of today then you are sadly mistaken!

Your primary task, as a selling agent, is to sell property on behalf of the seller, to find a purchaser who is not only willing, but *able* to complete the purchase, and to negotiate the highest possible price for the sale. However, if you are to achieve your goal, you must be prepared to offer far more practical help and advice than the agents of yesteryear.

Your clients will expect you to show expertise in the fields of mortgages, insurance and surveying, for example, all of which are specialist areas in their own right, and which will be discussed in greater detail later in this book.

Starting any new business venture requires careful planning and will benefit greatly if you already have several years' previous experience working within your chosen trade or profession. Estate agency is no exception, and at least some background knowledge of agency work is necessary. This book has been designed to provide that knowledge and to take the reader carefully through the process of starting up and running a profitable estate agency business specialising in the sale of private

Preface

residential property. It offers comprehensive and easy to follow guidelines, designed to ensure that the high quality of service now being demanded by the consumer is provided and maintained at all times.

Included throughout the book are a series of assignments to test your knowledge and application of the chapter content. These assignments also offer training material suitable for use by established agencies who wish their junior negotiators to undertake a training programme covering all the technical information and background knowledge essential in today's competitive property market. The assignments will complement any in-house training programme being undertaken by the student, and provide written material which can be assessed by trainers to ensure that the student reaches a high standard of achievement in all aspects of residential property negotiation.

Running Your Own Estate Agency contains all the information and guide-lines necessary to help you make successful sales and lay a sound foundation upon which a profitable business can grow and prosper.

It should be noted, however, that the information provided relates to the sale of property in England and Wales, and not in Scotland, where the law appertaining to property is somewhat different.

The male pronoun has been used throughout the book for stylistic reasons only. It covers both the masculine and feminine genders.

Chapter 1

Starting the Business

Introduction

There are many important decisions to be made when starting your own business, not least of which is whether to trade as a sole trader, a limited company or perhaps go into partnership with a colleague or friend.

Each has advantages and disadvantages, and each incurs its own responsibilities and legal obligations. Most estate agents begin their venture into the business world as sole traders, but it is important to understand the difference between each status before you decide which will be most suitable for you.

In this chapter we will be looking at the different ways in which you can establish your business, and how to prepare yourself, your office and your working methods ready to deliver an efficient and cost-effective service.

Sole trader

This is the most straightforward way of starting a business. You simply begin trading and any income made from the business is yours. However, as a sole trader you have unlimited personal liability for any debts incurred. This means that if your business should fail, you become responsible for paying off the debt, which could result in the loss of your home, your car and perhaps all your personal wealth.

Most sole traders work in their own businesses, but should you decide to employ a manager to run the business for you, and not work yourself, the financial responsibility still rests with you as the sole trader.

For tax purposes, you will be assessed as a self-employed person, and you will have to pay class 2 National Insurance contributions direct to the Department of Health and Social Security and class 4 National Insurance contributions through your tax assessment based on your business profits. Any business expenses, however, can be offset against your personal income and therefore it is important to retain accurate documentation of all financial transactions relating to the business so that assessment for income tax and Value Added Tax can be made.

As a sole trader or partner you are also able to offset any losses incurred during the first four years of trading against tax paid under the Pay As You Earn system during your previous employment. This amount will relate to the total amount of tax paid in the previous three years before you set up your business.

The limited company

By creating a limited company, you in effect become an employee of that company. In law, a limited company is considered to be a separate and independent unit quite apart from its owners. Its directors are the people who organise its business activities and make the decisions, and its owners are the people who have shares in it. In the event of the company failing, unlike the sole trader, these people are not personally liable for the company's debts, as claims are limited to the company's assets including any capital issued to shareholders.

Employees of a limited company must pay the required percentage (currently up to 9 per cent) of qualifying pay as National Insurance, and the company itself must pay the additional statutory percentage of employers' National Insurance contributions (currently up to 10.45 per cent of salary).

There are other legal obligations associated with starting a business as a limited company which are not required of the sole trader. A limited company, for instance, must file its annual audited accounts and other documents with the Registrar of Companies. It is also required to have a registered office and keep minutes of its directors' meetings.

A Memorandum of Association is required. This document sets out the purpose for which the business has been set up, states whether its registered office is in England, Scotland or Wales, and includes the maximum amount of authorised capital which can be put into the company. In addition to this, Articles of Association must also be drawn up. These indicate the rules laid down for the running of the business, the rights and responsibilities of the shareholders, together with the powers of directors. Although you can use your own, drawn up in conjunction with your solicitor, there are model articles laid down in the Companies Acts.

It is possible for a limited company to be owned by members of the public, or privately. A private company which cannot sell its shares to the public usually has a maximum of 50 members and a minimum of two, and must have at least one director. A public limited company must have a minimum of two members and at least one director. If you start trading as a sole trader and your business growth is such that additional capital is required, you could change to a limited company and so be in a position to sell shares to raise the extra capital you need. As a public company you may sell shares to the public, but you must have the required authorised capital.

In order to understand all these formalities properly, and implement the necessary procedures correctly, it is wise to seek the help and advice or your solicitor or accountant. Ultimately, however, you are responsible for ensuring that everything is carried out as it should be.

Partnerships

If you have no professional qualifications yourself, you may decide to start your business in partnership with someone who has some knowledge of the trade, or who has professional qualifications related to areas associated with property, such as surveying or finance.

Partners are much the same as sole traders. They are each entitled to a share of the profits, and are responsible for any debts incurred by the business. Each partner is also responsible for debts incurred by other partners, so if your partner disappears with all the money, you will be left to sort it all out. Unless the partners agree otherwise, a partnership can be regulated by the Partnership Act 1890.

An active partner works in the business as well as having financial responsibility, and a sleeping partner supplies capital and has a share of the profits, but does not take an active part in the running of the business.

In any business, good working relationships are essential. This is especially important in a partnership. Unfortunately, not every partnership runs as smoothly as it might, and you should arrange for your solicitor to draw up a partnership agreement to be approved by each partner involved.

The agreement should cover the following points:

- how decisions are to be made
- the individual responsibilities of each partner
- how financial matters are to be dealt with
- what procedure should be followed if a partner decides to withdraw from the partnership
- profit sharing
- the procedure to be undertaken in the event of the death of one of the partners
- procedure for dissolving the partnership if it should become necessary.

Raising the finance

For the small business, a loan from a bank in the form of an overdraft may well provide adequate funds to start trading. The interest rate charged on an overdraft is slightly above the bank's base lending rate, but is only charged on the amount which is overdrawn. Larger sums of money may be raised by way of a bank loan, however, or you could possibly arrange a package made up of part overdraft and part loan. Your bank manager is certainly the first person to approach to discuss the matter in full.

You will need to convince him that your business is going to be successful, especially if you have no previous track record, and to this end, with the help of your accountant if possible, you should draw up a carefully prepared *business plan* to present your case.

The plan should include the following points:

- details of all your previous business experience
- experience and previous background of anyone else involved in the business
- existing assets and liabilities
- full details of the service you propose to offer
- the area your service is likely to cover and how you propose to reach it
- the level of demand there is for your service
- the amount of competition you face
- how you intend to counter the competition by means of price, service or any other approach
- likely cost of premises and equipment required
- amount of loan required
- how the money will be used
- how much of your own money you propose to put into the business
- cash flow and profit and loss forecast for the first year's trading
- what security you can offer for the loan
- length of time the loan is needed for
- how you intend to pay it back.

The business plan must be as comprehensive as possible, while not being so long that the bank manager will need a week to read through it!

If you have no previous track record, you will need to persuade your bank manager that you have thought the whole matter through very carefully, and planned your moves in order to be progressive and profitable. He won't be convinced unless he feels there is a good chance that your business will make some sort of profit. After all, banks don't lend money unless they are fairly sure they can get it all back.

Starting the Business

You also need to do your homework carefully. Drive around the area you intend to work in and see how many For Sale and Sold boards are about. Check local agents' windows and local advertising in order to assess what level of demand there is likely to be for your business. Check out competitive companies and provide your bank manager with a comprehensive outline of how you intend to move into the market, advertise and make your presence felt.

Your figures will need to show the likely cost of office equipment and this should include:

- desks, chairs and other basic furniture
- fixtures and fittings
- filing cabinet
- good quality typewriter or word processor
- basic stationery
- camera
- dictaphone (optional)
- effective window display
- telephone and extensions as necessary
- photocopier (can be hired)
- For Sale boards of different sizes.

You will also have to submit a cash flow projection for the cost of premises and related charges, such as rent, rates, lighting and heating, and, of course, salaries and all your other ongoing overheads.

For the profit and loss forecast, your bank manager will expect you to show what financial position you expect to be in after the first year's trading. Selling property is not always easy to forecast, however. What you need to do is calculate your overall costs for the year, determine the average price of property in your area and from that the number of sales you will need to make in order to show a profit, based on the commission rate you intend to charge. You must then decide if the number of properties you need to sell relates to the number of properties which come up for sale during that period, and whether they are likely to be in a price range which will afford you the amount of commission you require to make ends meet as well as show a profit. You may need the help and advice of your accountant here, in order to present the figures accurately, and remember, too, that during the first few months of trading your income will be minimal. Not until sales start to complete will you receive any commission and adequate funding must be accounted for to tide you over this difficult period.

You must include details of your previous experience in selling, whether it is in the field of property or elsewhere, together with your managerial experience, if any, and details of any qualifications you have.

A carefully prepared curriculum vitae will serve the purpose well. If you are entering into a partnership, the same details will be required about your partner, or an indication of the background experience you will expect of any staff you intend to take on.

You will also need to explain the business and working methods you intend to adopt in order to paint an overall picture of what you intend to do and how you intend to do it.

Security for the loan can take many forms, the most common being the family home. If the property is jointly owned by husband and wife, then both parties must agree to the arrangement.

Present your business plan carefully. A few jotted notes are not sufficient. Type it or have it typed out and presented in an easy to read but comprehensive fashion. Some banks actually provide a checklist of the information they expect and the questions they will ask, but whatever bank you approach, make sure you know exactly what you are going to do, how you intend to do it and what financial position you will be in after one year of trading.

Enterprise Allowance

If you have been unemployed and receiving benefit for at least eight weeks, you could apply for the Enterprise Allowance via your local Jobcentre. If you are eligible, you will receive £40 per week for a period of a year, but you must show that you have a minimum of £1,000 to put towards the business yourself, and you must apply for the loan before you begin trading. However, aspiring estate agents are unlikely to be unemployed for such a period.

Private loans

You may be lucky enough to have friends or relatives willing to lend you money, but terms, conditions and interest rates must be agreed and confirmed in writing. The lender may wish to include a 'calling-in' clause which will specify the set period of notice he needs to give you if he requires the loan to be repaid in full.

You also need to establish that the lender has no claim on profits, or any rights in the running of the business, unless of course you particularly want him to. Your solicitor will draw up the necessary documentation and ensure that each party knows and fully understands his obligations with regard to the loan.

Buying an existing agency

Buying an established agency will give you the advantage of starting your business with an existing register of properties, rather than having to build up a register from scratch. However, the seller's books should be vetted by your accountant and you need to make sure you are not buying an agency which is unlikely to be profitable or is in an area where there are few properties likely to be for sale.

Business premises may be purchased or leased. If the premises are leased, check the terms and conditions of the lease, especially renewal clauses. Rent reviews are carried out at regular intervals at which times the landlord may increase the rent payable. You also need to know where the landlord's obligations end and yours begin, especially with regard to maintenance and insurance of the building. Some leases include the term 'full repairing and insuring' under which you are responsible for any repairs and maintenance as well as all the insurances. This could mean that you will be expected to repair any faults or damage to the building which were there before you took occupation. You will probably have to pay the landlord's legal costs too.

Although you may lease the premises, you will be purchasing the fixtures and fittings and the goodwill. As an estate agency, there will be no 'stock' as such, so you won't have that worry, but do check on any arrangements relating to the payment of fees for transactions that are currently under way, but which have not yet reached legal completion.

Remember that the agent's fee is only paid on completion of the transaction. The previous owner may have negotiated the sale, but completion may not take place until after you have purchased his business. In most cases, such commission becomes due to the new owner, as it is quite possible that he becomes instrumental in ensuring that completion of the sale is reached. Such an arrangement is of great benefit to the new owner, since completion may take place very shortly after the business is purchased. If you start a business from scratch, however, even if you sell a property on the very first day, completion probably won't take place until at least four weeks later. You therefore have to exist with no income during those early days, and this must be taken into account when you are budgeting for your new venture.

Choosing the right premises

There are many premises which can be used for commercial purposes. For the estate agent, it is essential to choose premises to which the public can obtain easy access, and where a window display can be shown to its best advantage.

Everyone is interested in property – especially property prices – and even if they have no intention of buying or selling at that particular time, most people find it hard to resist the temptation of peering into an agent's window as they pass by. It is therefore very important that you choose premises in a part of town where the public constantly pass by the window. Having an office on the top floor of a block, for instance, with no display facilities at ground floor level, is unlikely to invite many enquiries at all.

It is also very important to create an overall image of efficiency and professionalism, so choose your decor with care, but most importantly, create an eye-catching and well-lit window display. There is a variety of display systems currently available, and an investment in this area will certainly reap its full reward.

Extend your displays into the office as well. Use wall space for further photographs, maps and plans and, if finances allow, match your internal display system with that used for your window.

The layout of your office is also very important. Don't overclutter, so creating an untidy and shoddy impression. Your customers will assume the service you offer is also shoddy and uncaring. A carefully positioned display of plants can also enhance the appearance of your office, but coffee cups, full ashtrays and newspapers should *never* be seen.

You will need to invest in a photocopying machine suitable for reproducing specifications of properties to a very high standard. Don't accept one that creates black smudges and marks on otherwise crisp new headed stationery. Photocopiers can be leased, and you will find the names of suppliers in your local Yellow Pages.

There are a number of computer systems now available for the estate agent. Details of properties can be stored, together with mailing lists, customers' telephone numbers and so on. If your finances stretch to such a luxury, you will find it extremely beneficial. It is a simple matter to key in the specific requirements of a customer and produce details of all the properties which may be of interest. Systems can link offices, too, so that if a company has several branches, they may each have access to a central program. However, it has been known for information to be accidentally erased from a disc, so it is always a wise precaution to back up computerised information with simple written records.

You may even decide that a video system would be an advantage, finances allowing. Your customers will certainly be impressed if you are able to run a video showing each of the properties on your register.

The premises you choose, and the way you present them, say a great deal about you and your service, so choose with care. A small office with one good quality desk, and two or three carefully chosen chairs, creates a much more acceptable image than a large room, hastily filled with an assortment of tables and odd chairs. Don't lose customers just because they don't like the look of your office and don't bother to come in. Remember, you are in competition with many other agents, and today's property buyers and sellers are, and certainly have the right to be, very choosy indeed.

Health and Safety at Work Act 1974

It is essential that your premises comply with the conditions outlined in the Health and Safety at Work Act 1974. Your local Health and Safety Executive will supply leaflets and brochures setting out the requirements, and its inspector will confirm whether your premises meet those standards.

As an employer you are responsible for ensuring that your premises offer a safe and healthy working environment. You should have a safe working system and ensure that entrances and exits are safe and proper fire exits are available. Employees should be given training and information related to health and safety, and neither employees nor non-employees should be exposed to health or safety risks while on your premises. These are just a few of the many areas covered in the Act, and your local Executive will provide full details on request.

Planning permission

If you are buying an existing business you will need to check the terms of the planning consent relating to the premises. If *personal planning consent* was granted to the previous owner, it means that you must apply for planning consent yourself in order to continue to run the business along the same lines. The original personal planning consent which was granted meant that only the previous owner was able to use the building and its land for the purpose applied for.

If *temporary planning consent* was passed, then there was a time limit set on expiry of which planning permission must be sought again.

Full planning consent, however, means that the building and land can continue to be used for the purpose set out in the original consent document.

Starting from scratch means that planning permission must be obtained before you can open your new business. You will need to complete the appropriate forms and forward them to your local planning office together with plans of the premises. Don't forget that local surveyors can help you with all these matters, but they may not be anxious to do so if you intend to open your new office in competition with them, so you may prefer to consult your solicitor instead.

Insurance

Adequate insurance is another point not to be overlooked. Any reputable insurance company or insurance broker will give you advice on suitable insurance cover. Certain statutory insurances are required for all businesses, large and small, and these include employer's liability, motor vehicle insurance, public liability and building insurance. In the case of a partnership, all partners should be adequately insured in the event of the death of one partner. Other insurance cover will depend upon your personal and business circumstances.

If you act as an agent for a building society and could possibly have large sums of money on the premises, make sure suitable cover is secured. The building society will also consult you on this matter when the terms and conditions of the agency are agreed.

Offering mortgage facilities

It is absolutely essential that, as a selling agent, you are able to offer your customers help and advice when it comes to the important problem of obtaining a mortgage.

Many estate agents run building society agencies where customers can conduct their business in much the same way as if they were to go into a branch of their building society. The building society usually arrange to consider mortgage applications received from that agent on a priority basis. In some instances, they will even guarantee a loan subject to status. The terms and conditions of such an agreement must be negotiated with the building society. The society will arrange a suitable training programme if you take on this role, but you will be expected to provide adequate security measures for any monies you collect.

As an agent for a building society, you will be expected to undertake certain activities on their behalf. These will include:

- accepting money from customers to put into their accounts
- recording payments received in passbooks
- keeping accurate records of payments received
- issuing receipts for any passbooks to be forwarded direct to the parent company for any reason
- retaining a 'float' of a set amount of money if you undertake withdrawals from your agency
- ensuring that your records and cash balance at the end of each day
- undertaking proper banking procedures
- encouraging customers to open new accounts
- providing proper advertising for the building society.

Although terms and conditions vary, building societies usually pay commission to their agents, based on the amount of money paid into accounts, and the number and type of new accounts opened on their behalf. You may also be able to obtain financial assistance to improve and/or establish window and office frontage displays, usually under the condition that the building society is clearly advertised, together with the services it offers.

An active agency can therefore provide extra income as well as guaranteeing your clients preferential treatment when it comes to applying for mortgages.

Recent legislation allows building societies to act as selling agents, and some have taken up this option through established estate agencies. Banks and insurance companies have also recently moved into the field and are able to offer financial assistance to buyers through the estate agents who represent them. Many estate agents also offer in-house mortgage facilities for their clients. In order to compete at all, it is therefore essential for the smaller business to be able to secure mortgages for its customers.

A mutually acceptable arrangement with a mortgage broker could well help too. Your commission could be a percentage of the broker's commission or a set amount for each introduction which results in a completed transaction. Keep a record of every applicant you introduce to the broker, together with details of the mortgage arranged and the sum involved.

As an estate agent you may not be offering credit or hire yourself, but you could be arranging it for your customers through a building society, for which a consumer credit licence is required. Under the Consumer Credit Act 1974 it becomes a criminal offence to offer credit facilities without the appropriate licence. Specified in the Act are a number of categories for which a licence is required. Details of these can be obtained through the Trading Standards or Consumer Protection or Weights and Measures Departments of your local authority. It is important that you fully understand the categories for which a licence is needed, and that you obtain the licence before you engage in any of the activities included within the Act.

Although anyone can call himself an 'adviser' or a 'consultant' or anything else, since 1981 a *broker* must be a registered member of the Insurance Brokers' Registration Council. Brokers belong to the British Insurance Brokers' Association (BIBA) and the Corporation of Mortgage Brokers (CMB), and in June 1988, under the new Financial Services Act, all brokers must become members of the Financial Intermediaries', Managers' and Brokers' Regulatory Association (FIMBRA).

A broker will prefer to arrange an endowment mortgage linked to an insurance policy. His commission will be received from the insurance company and will be based on the premiums the policy-holder pays. He does not receive a commission if a straight repayment mortgage is placed, unless he also places an insurance policy such as mortgage protection. A reputable broker will not ask your customer to leave a non-returnable deposit of any kind.

Whatever mortgage facilities you are eventually able to offer, it is essential that you understand them fully, and have a thorough working knowledge of the constraints applied to advances by lenders (see Chapter 4 for full details). Leaflets and brochures are provided by most lenders which clearly outline the different types of mortgages offered. Repayment charts and tables of valuation/survey fees are also available, together with a variety of additional promotional material – all of which should be readily available for your customers.

Surveying services

If you are not a qualified surveyor yourself, you will need to be in contact with a local surveyor in order to draw on his particular expertise as and when it is required.

Where private surveys are requested by buyers, you should be in a position to introduce them to a qualified surveyor who is a member of the Royal Institution of Chartered Surveyors or the Incorporated Society of Valuers and Auctioneers. They can undertake the very popular House Buyer's Report and Valuation and Flat Buyer's Report and Valuation as well as full structural surveys and other services as outlined in Chapter 4.

Many buyers now seek confirmation that the property they are buying is correctly priced and value for money, and is in a good state of repair with no obvious structural defects – information which can be provided by the above reports. Advice on planning consent and specialist valuations can also be undertaken by a qualified surveyor.

Employing staff

Because of the nature of estate agency, you will be out of the office a great deal, measuring up property or taking prospective buyers to view, and it is therefore essential that at least one other person remains in the office ready to receive callers and continue the business during your absence. Your customers and clients are unlikely to be impressed if they continually find themselves talking to an answerphone, or arriving at an unmanned office. Buying property is a very important step in their lives and they have the right to expect you, or a member of your staff, to be on hand as and when required. Sales and instructions are easily lost if there is no initial contact point. Your customers will simply go to the agent down the road!

An efficient secretary who can double as an efficient negotiator is a boon to any small agency. Many agencies now remain open late at night and at weekends, so you may even consider taking on a part-time person to cover these times. Employing additional negotiators will certainly be necessary as your business expands and you will then have to think in terms of either a set annual salary or a basic salary plus commission on sales.

You may consider taking on a young person from the Youth Training Scheme. Trainees usually enrol on the scheme for a two-year training programme, during which they receive off-job training through their managing agent, and you – in conjunction with the managing agent – provide a comprehensive on-job training programme. This gives you the benefit of training someone in exactly the way you require and, as your business grows, giving that young person the opportunity of full-time employment if he or she meets your requirements. A small contribution towards their training allowance may be required. The remainder of their payment, plus travelling expenses over £3, is paid through their managing agent who also monitors and assesses their progress at regular intervals.

As soon as you employ staff you take on certain responsibilities and commitments. If you employ part-time staff, and their salary does not exceed the level at which PAYE must be deducted, then you will not have to pay the statutory National Insurance contribution.

PAYE must be deducted from wages by the employer, and paid to the Inland Revenue monthly. At the end of the tax year you will be required to issue to each employee form P60 detailing pay and tax deducted during the year, and you must forward to the Inland Revenue form P35 which is a summary of tax and graduated National Insurance contributions for all your employees for that year.

You are also required to issue each employee with a record of wages paid. This must indicate gross pay, net pay, details of any other payments, such as commission or overtime, and full details of all deductions made. This record or pay-slip must be issued on or before each pay-day, and you must keep a wages book recording all these details.

Should an employee leave, you must complete form P45. One part of this is retained by the employee and handed to his next employer; the other part is sent to the tax office.

As an employer, you are also responsible for paying statutory sick pay for the first 28 weeks of sickness, the amount of which depends on the average weekly earnings of the employee.

Statutory maternity pay, which was introduced in April 1987 also becomes your responsibility. The lower rate (fixed annually: £34.25 per week 1988–89) is paid for 18 weeks after the employee leaves, if she was employed from 26 weeks to two years. The higher rate (nine-tenths of average weekly wage) is paid for the first six weeks' entitlement, the lower rate for 12 weeks if she was employed over two years.

The Inland Revenue issue several leaflets explaining these and other points in great detail, and these can be obtained from your local office free of charge.

Employment contracts

Each employee should be issued with a contract of employment. This should clearly set out the employee's job title and the tasks involved. It must include full details of salary, holidays, sickness pay, hours of business, pension scheme details, disciplinary and grievance procedures, length of notice required, in fact everything relating to the position offered. A copy should be signed by the employee to signify his acceptance of the contract, and although this may seem something of a headache to the employer, it is certainly a worthwhile and sensible document, designed to clarify the position of both employer and employee.

We have already mentioned how important an efficient secretary can be to the smaller agency, so let us look at an example of the job description you might draw up to include in the contract of employment:

JOB TITLE	Secretary/in-house negotiator
EMPLOYER	(your business name and address)
RESPONSIBLE TO	(yourself)
HOURS	(working hours including details of any special arrangements for covering late evenings or weekend work if this is likely)
DUTIES	**ADMINISTRATION**
	typing all correspondence and specifications; maintaining and updating all filing systems; undertaking photocopying duties to ensure that adequate supplies are always available; responsible for arranging development, and re-ordering, of photographs for specifications and displays as and when necessary; responsible for ordering and maintaining stocks of stationery; responsible for maintaining and updating mailing lists; responsible for recording and distributing outgoing and incoming mail;

responsible for administration of building society agency, balancing monies received or paid out to customers, banking and security of same;

responsible for ensuring that accurate records are maintained at all times in line with in-house record-keeping systems;

responsible for ensuring that all displays are updated and accurate;

in the absence of (yourself or other negotiators in your employ) administrating procedure for placing advertisements, maintaining records of advertisements placed and monitoring response;

DEALING WITH CUSTOMERS

receiving incoming telephone calls and dealing effectively with enquiries;

receiving customers and providing information as required in the absence of (yourself or other negotiators in your employ);

in the absence of (yourself or other negotiators in your employ) following up mailing list data, viewings, ongoing sales, possible valuations;

responsible for ensuring that all appointments made for or with customers are confirmed and accurately recorded;

in the absence of (yourself or other negotiators in your employ) undertaking negotiations for sales, and liaising with customers and clients to secure sales and instructions;

SPECIAL RESPONSIBILITIES

responsible for providing and maintaining an efficient service at all times;

responsible for reporting all activities to (yourself);

responsible for ensuring that no activity is undertaken which may be detrimental to the business or (yourself) or to other members of staff;

HEALTH AND SAFETY AT WORK

show knowledge and understanding of the Health and Safety at Work Act, and ensure that working methods are in no way hazardous to either employees or customers;

understand and apply appropriate fire precautions.

As you can see, the tasks outlined above are varied and represent many areas which you will be unable to cover while out of the office. If your secretary also undertakes simple negotiations in your absence, it could clinch those sales and instructions that might otherwise have been lost. You must remember, though, that you have overall responsibility for everything that goes on in your office, and you should only delegate tasks to members of staff who are capable of carrying them out efficiently.

Dismissing staff

A small company is unlikely to be sued for unfair dismissal. Even if you should find yourself in this unhappy position, an industrial tribunal must take into account the size of your company and whether or not you acted 'reasonably'.

Employees qualify for protection against unfair dismissal only after they have been with the firm for two years provided the employer has at no time employed more than 20 employees. If more than 20 people have been employed, then the employee qualifies after only one year. A pregnant woman does not have the right to insist on reinstatement if you employ less than five people.

If it is necessary for you to dismiss members of staff, you should do so with discretion and, of course, only with good reason. A verbal and/or written warning of dismissal should be given and the reasons for it made quite clear. Misconduct, poor timekeeping or incompetence are admissible reasons for dismissal. Redundancy, however, occurs when there is no job to be filled, and statutory redundancy pay becomes due to employees over the age of 18 who have been continuously employed for a minimum period of two years.

Value Added Tax

A business with an annual turnover of over £22,100 or £7,500 in any one quarter must register with Customs and Excise and it will be issued with a VAT registration number. VAT is in fact chargeable for services as well as goods and, having registered, every quarter you must submit 15 per cent of the charges you have made, less any VAT charges made to you for supplies purchased. This entails very careful record keeping, so make sure you know how your accountant expects such records to be maintained.

What makes a profit?

As we discussed earlier, the traditional method of estate agency comes under the heading 'No Sale, No Fee'. The fee becomes payable to the agent who first introduces the buyer to the property, and is paid by the seller on completion of the transaction, which could well be some considerable time after the sale was originally negotiated and agreed. No charge is made for work carried out in respect of any negotiations which do not result in legal completion.

There is in fact no set scale of fees. They are negotiable. However, most agents charge between 1 and 3 per cent of the eventual selling price of the property. Lower fees are charged if a *sole agency* is agreed, this being when you are the only agent acting on behalf of the seller. The terms and conditions under which these fees become due are explained in greater detail in Chapter 4.

Over the last few years we have seen the introduction of different methods of selling property, including property shops and computer sales. These types of business usually charge a set fee to the seller when he registers his property as being for sale. This fixed amount is paid whether or not a sale is forthcoming. Solicitors, too, are now able to act as selling agents for their clients, and most set a special charge inclusive of all the legal work undertaken in respect of the sale.

If you run your business along traditional lines, your total income depends upon the number of successful sales which you negotiate, plus any commission or introduction fees received in respect of placing mortgages or running a financial agency. Regardless of how much effort and expense has gone into a negotiation, if it does not complete, no financial reward can be claimed. Forward planning and careful financial control are therefore essential. Your accountant will advise you how he requires records of accounts to be maintained, but what you must budget for is that long period between starting your business and receiving your first commission cheque. During that time, your overheads and running costs must still be paid as and when required, and don't overlook essential advertising costs.

Keeping the books

It is essential in any business to keep a careful record of all your financial activities. We have already mentioned a wages book, and a cash analysis book, showing full details of your expenditure together with full details of your income, is another important record to maintain. You should also keep a simple petty cash book in the office to show all the minor expenses incurred for such things as postage, tea or coffee and other small sums.

Your cash analysis book should be divided into two main sections headed income and expenditure. Sub-divisions should include date, nature of income or expenditure and total amount paid or received, VAT paid or received, and separate headings for wages, advertising, running cost of premises including repairs and insurance, stationery, postage, telephone and any other break-down of total you wish to monitor. At the end of the month it is an easy matter to cast an eye along each column and see exactly how much money has gone out of the business and for what, and how much money has been received.

You must, of course, keep bank statements and a record of cheques received and paid into your account, together with receipts for all purchases so that figures can be checked.

Your accountant will draw up a profit and loss account from the record books you maintain, and in the case of a limited company, a balance sheet must be drawn up at the end of your financial year and forwarded to the Registrar of Companies.

Many estate agents and small businesses generally employ part-time bookkeepers for a few hours a week to keep records and deal with pay, and if you have difficulty getting to grips with the paperwork, this could well solve your problem. However, audited accounts must be submitted by a professionally qualified accountant who is a member of either the Institute of Chartered Accountants or the Chartered Association of Certified Accountants.

The Board of Inland Revenue issue a very comprehensive booklet, reference IR28, called 'Starting in Business', which contains an outline of tax procedures and advice on related record keeping, and includes the following:

- things to do at the outset
- partnerships
- engaging an accountant
- employees
- choice of accounting date
- preparation of accounts
- books and records
- income tax profit
- capital expenditure
- business expenditure
- Enterprise Allowance
- basis of assessment of income tax
- assessments, appeals and payment of tax
- classes 2 and 4 National Insurance contributions.

There is also a form at the back of the booklet – form 41G – which you need to complete to register your company for tax purposes. Also included is a list of other pamphlets and publications together with sources from which they can be obtained. Your local tax office will supply a copy of the booklet, free of charge.

The decision to move from the reasonable security of being an employee into the world of the self-employed is not one to be taken lightly. A great deal of planning and careful budgeting is required. But bear in mind that your accountant, solicitor and bank manager are there to offer all the help and guidance you need, especially when it comes to efficient bookkeeping.

Technical colleges and further education centres also run a variety of courses specifically for those entrepreneurs starting in business on their own, all with the same problems, all with the same ambition – to show a profit and to succeed in their businesses.

By joining such a group you will have the support and help of others, and the opportunity to share experiences and exchange ideas as well as some comprehensive help and advice on basic bookkeeping techniques. You can then progress to more advanced bookkeeping if you wish.

Your business name

An estate agent must present a professional image. The name you choose for your business should reflect, if possible, your attitude and ideas. The name 'Country Properties', for instance, gives the impression that the type of properties you specialise in are all in a country location, and someone looking for a small flat in the middle of town is unlikely to approach you. Many agents simply use their own name, which is fine as long as you indicate that you are in fact trading as an estate agent and not a fishmonger.

The compulsory registration of business names was abolished in January 1982; however, there are still certain rules which apply. If you decide not to trade under your own name, your name and the names of any partners you have must be shown on all your business documents and must be prominently displayed on your premises as required by Section 29 of the Companies Act 1981. A limited company must display its registration number, address of its registered office and names of its directors, and if you are asked for this information in relation to any of your business dealings, you must disclose it in writing. You are committing a criminal offence if you fail to do so.

The importance of image

Image can be greatly enhanced by logos and colour schemes, and there are many companies which specialise in creating overall images for specific businesses, large and small.

The design and colour of your stationery should extend to all your advertising material, especially For Sale boards, and your logo should appear as often as possible.

You will need the following basic stock of stationery:

- letter headings
- business cards
- compliments slips
- specification headings for details of properties and, if possible, a matching folder in which to present the details, produced on good quality paper or card
- invoices
- pro formas: this form is a detailed account of an agreed sale and must include:
  - full address of the property sold
  - agreed purchase price
  - whether the property is leasehold or freehold
  - terms and conditions of the lease if leasehold
  - vendor's full name and telephone number (home and business) and address if different from property sold
  - name and address of vendor's solicitor
  - buyer's full name, address and telephone number (home and business)
  - name and address of buyer's solicitor
  - buyer's financial arrangements including:
    name of lender if mortgage is required
    full details of mortgage arrangements
    or cash
    or bridging finance
  - amount of deposit paid, if any
  - if buyer has a property to sell, full details of the chain if there is one
  - anticipated completion date
  - any other special notes about the transaction
- local maps to present to applicants: contact the Ordnance Survey department to check copyright conditions, and you may find other local traders prepared to contribute towards the cost in return for their advertisement appearing somewhere on the document.

Window displays

It is absolutely essential that your window display is perfect. A clear colour photograph of each property should be displayed, and where an internal view or view of the garden might be an added attraction, this should also be included. If you have limited space, choose a window display which presents details of properties designed to encourage enquiries and entice prospective buyers into your office to see what else you have to offer.

Make sure that as soon as a property is sold, or there is a price change for some reason, your window display is updated and changed accordingly. Never leave old or faded photographs in a window, or forget to change or update information. Customers get extremely annoyed if you clearly show a property as being for sale and, on making enquiries, they find it was sold three weeks earlier. Vendors, to whom your first obligation lies, will also not be happy if they find you displaying incorrect information about their property, and showing photographs which do nothing to encourage prospective buyers to view.

Your displays must be kept clean and dust free – no dead flies – and brochures advertising any additional services you offer should not be left to fade and discolour. One or two strategically placed, excellently presented photographs are far more eye-catching than too many, too small and too tightly packed. Although you may not be a professional photographer, your customers will still expect professional quality, so it is worth investing in a good camera.

Lighting is another important point. A well-lit window display both during the day, as well as the evening and at weekends, is essential. You can have a timer fixed to the lighting system so that it remains on during the evening, when many people browse and window-shop, but turns off later at night.

Your window says a lot about you. Don't let it let you down. Keep it clean and make sure the exterior is properly painted and in good condition. A great number of people will notice.

Advertising

If you look at any local newspaper advertising property, you will immediately be drawn to the photographs. So, too, will anyone looking for a property to buy.

Of course, including photographs in advertising material increases your advertising costs enormously. However, if you are to compete with multi-branch businesses who display complete pages of advertising material, then you must be prepared to spend money. It is not an area where cost-cutting pays off.

Local newspapers will draw up suitable artwork for you, including logos or any special surround or feature required. Each time you place an advertisement, these details will then be included. Once you have hit upon a successful layout, stick to it. The consumer will soon relate it to you, and will respond to it each time it appears.

Any properties which have just come on to your books should be immediately advertised. So should any property with a change of price. Sellers will also be checking the paper to ensure that you are including their homes, so make sure the description you give is accurate and emphasises any special points which will encourage enquiries.

Advertising is such an essential part of the estate agent's world that it must receive proper care and attention, and each advertisement must be carefully chosen for its content and to ensure that a range of properties is included. This will encourage enquiries for all types of properties, in all price ranges. From these enquiries you can then introduce the customer to other properties on your register similar in price to the one advertised, thus ensuring that each person who makes an enquiry receives details of every property on your register which may be of interest, even those not advertised at the time.

From an agent's point of view, successful advertising is an acquired skill. Choosing the right property to advertise and the right price ranges to include really becomes an art, and you will soon see, if you monitor the response to each of your advertisements, which layout or content produces the most enquiries and subsequent sales.

The more expensive the property, the more commission you will receive if you conclude a sale, hence the ability to lavish more funds on advertising higher priced properties. However, don't overlook the cheaper properties, which should be easier to sell anyway.

You may argue that as they are easy to sell, they do not require an advertisement, but remember, your advertisement is to encourage a range of enquiries, and if you only advertise expensive properties, readers may assume that you do not deal in the smaller, less expensive type. You will soon find enquiries dwindling away and quick turnover properties no longer coming on to your register.

Regular advertising is another essential ingredient. It is no good advertising once in a blue moon. People will soon forget you exist. You must advertise on a regular basis and implant yourself on the memory of the reader, so that when he eventually decides to instruct a selling agent, yours is the first name that comes to mind.

The wording and content of your advertisement are also important. Avoid jargon if possible and don't waste expensive advertising space on trivia. Emphasise what is best about the property. Always include area and price, and don't be misled into believing that if you leave out the price you will get more enquiries. People will assume you are either inefficient, the property is overpriced or there is some trickery afoot and they won't bother to ring at all.

Humorous advertisements may be outstanding, but they do not always reflect a professional approach, and most vendors are unimpressed if you make fun of their property.

Make sure you use all the advertising outlets available. Not only local newspapers, but posters and suitable magazines. If you are about to open your agency, arrange a leaflet drop in the area which, although it may not include specific properties, should detail all the services you can offer, and let everyone know you are there! Make sure you include a telephone number where you can be contacted immediately, so that if they have a property to sell, arrangements can be made for you to measure up right away. You need to build up your register of properties as soon as possible, and this is an excellent way of launching yourself into the property world. You may even offer a special reduced fee during the first few weeks of opening the business.

Creative advertising is an essential part of estate agency. Time and care spent on it will undoubtedly be worthwhile.

Boards

For Sale boards, and especially Sold boards, are another essential form of advertising for the agent. Not only does a For Sale board invite enquiries, but it also establishes the name of the agent firmly in the mind of all the potential house sellers in the area. Follow it with a Sold notice, and when they come to sell their homes, they will certainly remember you.

The design of your board should incorporate your business logo and reflect any colour pattern you have chosen for your stationery and/or office decor. It should be simple but explicit. Your name and telephone number are the most important features, the address of your office coming second. Your boards should be so clear that anyone driving by can catch your name and telephone number quickly.

Not all sellers want a For Sale board in their garden, but from your point of view it is an excellent advertising medium, and from their point of view it could well attract that special buyer who might otherwise be looking elsewhere. It is up to you to persuade the seller to allow you to place a board, as long as doing so remains in line with any planning or other restrictions which apply to the property. Some agents do this by offering a slightly reduced commission percentage, or perhaps a reduction of a fixed amount. Obviously this is not the best course of action, but it is worth considering if there is no other avenue open to you.

You may wish to erect boards yourself or employ someone to maintain and erect them for you. Whichever you choose, it is most important to keep a careful check on the properties which have boards, and ensure that they are collected at the appropriate time and not left to rot behind someone's garage. Sold and Under Offer stickers can be attached to For Sale boards, and another important point is to make sure the board is securely erected in a prominent but *very safe* position.

Boards can be produced in a variety of shapes and sizes. The 'flag' type is always popular, but larger display boards which can be attached to fences and walls, or erected in more open areas, are a necessary addition to your collection. Special circumstances may well require special boards to be produced, and large window stickers can be used for flats where it is not practical to erect a board.

Proposed legislation governing the size and number of boards which estate agents can display outside property has been considered inappropriate by the National Association of Estate Agents. However, the Association have been monitoring the situation closely and they feel that many of the problems stem from over-enthusiasm on the part of agents rather than the size of the boards generally. Concern has been voiced about the use of multiple boards outside a property or block of flats, boards being left outside property which has been sold, dangerously erected boards, and boards displayed outside property which is not for sale.

The Association have put forward a scheme suggesting a reduction in the maximum size of boards to 2.5×3 ft as opposed to the 2.5×2 ft suggested in the legislation. They also suggest that breach of planning regulations by the erection of multiple boards should be made undesirable practice under the Estate Agents Act 1979, and that fines should be imposed on agents who breach the restrictions. They also suggest that the offending agent be banned from displaying any boards at all for a period of up to six months thereafter.

In the light of these events, you must make sure that the boards you erect are in line with regulations laid down by your own local authority and follow the sensible course of action outlined by the Association.

The importance of first contact

Your first contact with customers will be either on the telephone or when they come into your office. At that point you must make a good impression.

A professional telephone manner from every member of your staff is essential. Answering the telephone in an estate agent's office is not a job for the office junior. You must be positive. You must know your register of properties inside out. You must be fully conversant with each negotiation which is presently under way, and if advertisements have been placed, you must have every detail immediately to hand. Slow, uncertain and hesitant responses to telephone enquiries can lose a sale. *Never* keep a customer waiting on the telephone.

You must always assume that the people calling you in response to an advertisement will also be calling other agents. The way you approach the enquiries, therefore, must reflect your knowledge and willingness to give customers every assistance possible. They could well receive details of the same property from several agents. The agent they will come back to, however, will be the one who offers the most help and advice.

Your approach to customers coming into your office must be just as professional and thorough. We have already discussed the overall image the presentation of your office can produce, but you too are part of that image – as is every member of your staff.

Customers must never be left unattended. Even if you are on the telephone, a smile of acknowledgement and a gesture towards a chair or a display of photographs will assure customers that they are not being neglected.

Have property magazines and brochures displayed around the office so that your customers can browse if you cannot speak to them immediately.

Always remember that every enquiry is a potential sale and/or instruction to sell, and that the commission paid by sellers is due to the agent who *first* introduces a property to a buyer. Don't lose business by underestimating the importance of that first contact with your customer.

Business growth by recommendation

Much of the reputation gained by an estate agent is built on recommendation. An agent who has produced a quick and successful sale, and helped and advised customers throughout their negotiations, will be remembered and talked about. However, although people will sometimes offer praise, they are much quicker to criticise, and if the service offered has not been what your customer expected, he will certainly mention it to his neighbour, who will mention it to his neighbour, and so on.

Estate agency is built on reputation. If you make a successful sale now, the customer you dealt with will come back to you again when he next moves home, and so future business is forthcoming. Make a mistake and you immediately lose that business. One very successful agent continues to send Christmas cards to every person who has bought property from him. An additional expense yes, but it has proved a very successful ploy. If any of his ex-customers talk about agents, his name is the one they remember.

Efficient record keeping

You cannot hope to run a successful agency unless you maintain efficient records. You will be dealing with many properties, and each will have many different people associated with it. Careful record keeping is therefore essential.

Your diary
You must *never* be late for an appointment. Under no circumstances is it acceptable to keep a customer waiting. Apart from being extremely rude, it shows lack of interest and lack of professionalism. It is the quickest way to lose business. If you make appointments, make sure you have the full address, the correct name – never arrive at a property not knowing the name of the person you are supposed to be meeting – and a telephone number. Make sure that each member of staff knows exactly where you are at any one time, and the name of the person you are with.

You could have a central diary in which all appointments for every member of staff are recorded, or a separate diary for each person. If separate diaries are maintained, make sure everyone knows what everyone else is doing so that a situation cannot arise where all the negotiators are out of the office together for any length of time. Also ensure that adequate time is allowed for each appointment. Your customers will not be impressed if you keep looking at your watch and do not give them your undivided attention.

Daybooks
A daybook is a complete record of every telephone call, every message, every activity undertaken throughout the day. It is one of the most essential records in any estate agent's office. Each activity should be recorded in detail, together with a note of the time it took place. Although this may well seem an unnecessary chore for the beginner, you will soon find, as your business grows, just how important an accurate daybook can be. It will give you a master copy of names, addresses, telephone numbers, appointments made, price changes, instructions received – in fact, a master copy of everything that has gone on during the day.

Because negotiating sales and purchases is such a complex business, it is very easy for misunderstandings to arise. All too often we hear of chains of sales and purchases falling through, and it is usually the agent involved who is blamed for not taking messages, or checking out facts, and so on. Your daybook, if it is maintained efficiently, will record such messages and facts, and it will be easy to check back on information received. All relevant information should then be transferred to other records as appropriate, still leaving the daybook as your master copy.

File notes
Everyone in the office must be in a position to find information relating to every property and every sale currently being dealt with. Although one

person may have overall responsibility for a transaction, other members of staff must be able to find out what is going on in his absence. To this end, file notes can be extremely helpful, and should contain a step-by-step record of every contact, every message and every move made so far, and should be retained in the file to which they refer.

Viewing card index

It is helpful to have on your desk a record of every property on your register with the name and telephone number of the vendor and instructions for making viewing arrangements, together with a brief description of the property itself. Many agents have folio numbers for each property registered, and viewing cards can be kept in folio, alphabetical or, better still, price order. You can use simple postcards stored in a small box on your desk, or any other suitable medium which is easily accessible and which does not require you to wade through a complete filing cabinet in order to find the information you want – especially when there are customers waiting.

Viewing books

It is essential that every viewing appointment made is followed up by a telephone call in order to find out the viewer's response. Even if you have taken someone to view a property, you should follow this up with a telephone call to find out what reaction has been forthcoming and report back to the vendor. This is especially important if the vendor does not actually live in the property and you hold a key for viewing purposes. Unless you keep in close contact with your clients, they will have no idea what action you are taking on their behalf, or what response there is towards effecting a sale. They may even think you are doing absolutely nothing, withdraw the property from your register and instruct another agent.

Although details of each viewing should be recorded as file notes, a separate viewing book is extremely helpful. A record of the name, address and contact telephone number of the viewer should be made, together with the address of each property he views, who made the appointment and for what time, whether it was an escorted viewing or not, and, of course, a note of the follow-up call and the viewer's response.

A great deal can be learnt from effective follow-up. You may find that the type of property the applicant actually wants is not at all like the one you sent him to view, in which case you can redirect his interest to something more suitable. You may even find that he has told the seller he wants to purchase, but has so far omitted to tell you! Unfortunately, too, people left to make their own way to view a property very often don't keep their appointments, and it will be your responsibility to explain to the vendor why you didn't put yourself out to take the viewer to the property, and why the vendor was left waiting anxiously at the window.

Mailing lists

Many agents are reluctant, or simply don't bother, to keep in contact with people who have enquired about property either in response to advertisements or by direct personal contact. Yet, as we have already said, *every* enquiry is a potential sale and/or instruction to sell – if not now, then some time in the future.

Mailing lists are therefore an integral part of estate agency work. Customers expect you to keep them informed of property as it comes on to the market, and although some may argue that agents send brochures of properties which are not at all what they requested, it at least shows that the agent is interested in their needs. Here, again, careful follow-up procedures should be undertaken.

Your mailing lists should include a telephone number for your applicant, and it is a wise agent who takes the opportunity to speak to customers a few days after sending out brochures, to monitor their response. Viewing arrangements and subsequent sales can often be negotiated, and this contact also gives you the opportunity to discuss the possibility of a valuation, or even an instruction to sell.

By maintaining contact with applicants, you are also in a position to keep your mailing list up to date. If you contact your applicant regularly, he will be quick to tell you if he is no longer looking for a property to buy, or if perhaps he has purchased elsewhere. If this should be the case, then you may discreetly enquire what he has purchased and where, and this gives you the ideal opportunity to assess the current competition from other agents. If by any chance the applicant has purchased a property from another agent, and that same property is on your register, then somewhere along the line something has gone drastically wrong and you must immediately check your daybook and other records to try to establish how you missed the sale.

It is up to you to keep in touch. You are unlikely to find many applicants making the effort to let you know they are suited unless you approach them directly.

Computerised mailing lists are the ideal way of maintaining an up-to-date list, but simple record cards containing all the applicant's details, together with details of each property sent, serve the purpose just as well. Typing envelopes is something of a chore, especially as it is essential to send out brochures immediately instructions to sell have been finalised, but an efficient and reliable typist should be able to work quickly enough to catch the latest post.

Other systems for printing out names and addresses for mail-shots are available, however, and suppliers can be located through your local Yellow Pages.

As soon as you receive instructions to sell a property, check your mailing list and telephone all those customers who might be interested, with a view to making an immediate viewing appointment. You might even keep a separate 'hot list' of those applicants who are in a position to complete a purchase immediately. Many sales are tied up this way, even before the property has been advertised.

Sales record book

A sales record book should be designed to show, at a glance, all your negotiated sales, together with commission due and commission paid. It should be divided into months and include the following:

- address of property
- name and address of seller
- name and address of buyer
- agreed purchase price
- commission due
- date of exchange of contracts
- invoice number
- completion date
- commission received and date.

Such a record book will provide an easy way to see exactly how many sales have been negotiated, how much commission is due and how much commission has been paid to date.

Is all the information there?

We have been looking at the different procedures for record keeping in the estate agent's office, and you will no doubt have your own system as well. The secret is to have to hand every piece of information available so that all members of staff who might receive a telephone call, or deal with a personal caller, can obtain the relevant details without keeping anyone waiting. This must include part-time staff or weekend staff who will need to find out exactly what has been going on in their absence in order to deal effectively with any enquiry they may receive.

Why should customers choose you?

At this stage you must sit back and analyse exactly what services you can offer, and what image you project, to persuade buyers and sellers to contact you rather than your competitors.

Vendors will expect the agent they employ to present accurate and well-displayed specifications of their property, and to ensure that everyone on the mailing list receives a copy immediately the property is put on the market. They will expect each copy to contain a colour photograph, and they expect to see a photograph of their property prominently displayed in your window. They will also want to see their property advertised in the press, and will most certainly expect you to bring prospective viewers around as soon as possible. If you don't, they will expect, and deserve, an explanation. However, they will not want you to pester them with viewers who are time-wasters, or who are not in a position to complete the purchase even if they wanted to.

You will need to spend time going through specifications with your applicants, taking them to view property, providing them with a map and any other information they need about the area in general, and offer help and advice on matters such as mortgages. If asked, you must be prepared to give an indication as to how much legal, survey and other fees are likely to be, at the same time treating each enquiry in the strictest confidence.

Buyers and sellers will only choose you if you can provide these services, if they are impressed with the standard of your advertising and have no doubt about the efficiency of your business methods.

Conclusion

In this chapter we have looked at the steps necessary to establish your agency, and the steps necessary to encourage people to bring their business to you rather than to other agents in your area. We have seen how important it is that you are aware of, and can therefore deal effectively with, competition from other selling agents, and if at this early stage you are unable to lavish a great deal of money on pages of house advertisements, remember that it is *quality* that counts.

As in any new business venture, it is essential that competition in the field is assessed and analysed. Check the territory you cover to find out who displays the most boards, and monitor advertisements too. Be *aware* of the competition and you will be able to deal with it.

Although you may well have reservations and doubts at this early stage of your new career, bear in mind that as an estate agent there is something very special about handing over the keys of a property to its new owner. Making the sale may not have been easy, but nevertheless it was successful and no doubt, in a few years' time, that new owner will be coming back to you, asking you to sell the property again, as he moves on to bigger and better things. That's what agency work is all about, and that's what makes it all so very worthwhile.

Assignment 1: Assessing the competition

Objectives
- To evaluate the level of service offered by competitors in your area
- To identify areas where your own image and level of service could be improved and become more efficient

Tasks

1. Make a list of all the services available to buyers and sellers through other agencies in your area and identify any which you are unable to offer. Explain why this is so and what your company could do in order to compete.
2. Tour the area and identify from the number of boards which company appears to be the most active, and which properties with boards you do not have on your own register.
3. Study advertisements placed by other agents and identify which agent offers the most variety of properties and presents the most effective display.
4. Compare your own advertisements with others and identify areas where you could improve display, content or general appearance in order to encourage more replies.
5. Monitor your advertisements over a period of four weeks, changing layout and format, and ascertain which receives the most satisfactory response and why.
6. Produce a flow chart showing each element of your record-keeping system, and how messages, information and other details are incorporated into the system. From that chart, identify any points where important information could be lost, or where additional record keeping might be advantageous.
7. If you are training with a larger company, produce an organisation chart showing each member of staff and his or her role within the company. Produce a corresponding flow chart showing how you work together to produce a sale. Your chart should identify who would deal with the customer at the point of first contact, and how many other staff would be involved with that customer until completion.
8. From your charts, identify any weak links in your inter-office communication system which could result in customers not seeing the right person at the right time, or where customers might be kept waiting because the information required is not immediately available to the member of staff they are speaking to.

9. Provide a written report offering constructive ideas for improving record-keeping methods or inter-staff communication where you feel this is necessary, and say how such improvements would affect the service your company offers to its customers.

Chapter 2

The Art of Good Salesmanship

Introduction

To some people, the art of successful selling – whatever the commodity – comes quite easily. To others, it is an acquired skill, perfected only after sound training and considerable practical experience.

For the estate agent the art of successful selling relies not only on excellent selling skills, but skills in the art of counselling, listening and interpreting, coupled with unquestionable product knowledge and infinite patience. Because the business of buying and selling property is a very complex and personal one, a successful agent must be prepared to perfect all these skills if he hopes to negotiate sales which will not fall through.

In this chapter we will look at those skills, and see how they should be put into practice.

Identifying your customer's needs

Each time you receive an enquiry from a prospective purchaser, it is necessary to determine, as far as possible, what type of property that customer will eventually purchase. Agents have long since discovered that, in many cases, the property their customers eventually buy is not at all like the property they originally requested.

In the previous chapter we discussed how important it is to encourage enquiries for all types of property and in all price ranges. When you receive enquiries, however, you may well find that the details requested are not at all in line with what the customer can actually afford, or what would be most suitable for him.

A four-bedroomed property on an estate, for instance, is unlikely to be the most suitable choice for a couple whose own family have grown up and left home. Four-bedroomed properties are obviously family homes, and there will be children about, cars coming and going, and all the usual activities of a bustling household: not altogether suitable for a couple looking for a tranquil and quiet place to retire.

Equally, a young couple with little or no deposit to put towards the purchase may not be able to buy an old property in need of extensive maintenance and repair work unless its value reaches the amount of the loan required. They probably don't know that lenders require the property to be of a certain value and standard before they will advance a very high percentage of the total purchase price.

These are, of course, only examples, but they show the type of situation where a negotiator who has not applied any thought to the case might arrange for a purchase to proceed, only to find in a few weeks' time that our older couple have purchased a retirement home or a smaller property from someone else, and our young couple have been refused a mortgage and have gone to another agent who has since shown them a more suitable property for mortgage purposes.

Many of the problems which result in sales falling through because customers are unable to obtain mortgages, or simply change their minds, are caused because the negotiator has not identified the customer's needs correctly.

There are certain basic questions you need to ask every time you receive an enquiry, either by telephone or by personal contact, the answers to which should be retained on mailing list records for future reference:

Example
Name
Address
Telephone number for immediate contact both at home and at workplace
Price range
Brief details of type of property required
Location preferred
If the customer is a first-time buyer:
- has he arranged a mortgage in principle?
- what percentage of price is likely to be required on mortgage?
- if no mortgage arrangements have been made, can you help?
If the customer has a property to sell:
- is the property currently on the market?
- is it sold subject to contract?
- if so, is there a chain involved (take *full* details)?
- what time factor is involved?
- if there is no sale agreed, can you act as selling agent?
- how much response has there been so far?
Any other comments:

From these brief details you can soon build up an overall picture of your customer's purchasing capability.

If the customer has a property to sell, you should be able to secure his instructions and act as agent for him. If he has already sold, however, it is necessary to find out as much as you possibly can about any chain which is involved. A chain can be linked by just two people, or many, in which case if just one of them has a problem, the whole chain could break down. If there is any doubt, just take the name of the agent who sold the property and you will always have a contact point to check out details. The seller's solicitor will also be in a position to confirm facts, so it is helpful to know which solicitor is involved.

It will be of little use to agree a sale to someone who is not in a position to complete quickly, if this is what the seller requires. You would not be acting in the best interests of the seller if you concluded the sale without doing your homework thoroughly.

Every enquiry is potential business

Every enquiry is a potential sale or instruction to sell and should be treated as such.

Any commission due on a sale is payable to the agent who *first* introduced the client to the property. Therefore it is very important to keep accurate records of each specification you have given out and to whom. Wherever possible, arrange to take your applicants to see the property right away, so there is no possibility of them obtaining the particulars of the same property from another agent, and making viewing arrangements through that agent, leaving you with a lost sale.

There is always the possibility, too, of the applicant receiving particulars from you, not making viewing arrangements, but calling to see the property anyway and trying to negotiate privately with the seller, leaving you out altogether.

Because this sometimes happens, you must make sure you have a complete list of all the details given. If you receive a call from a seller to say his property has been sold and he no longer wishes you to act on his behalf, it is a wise precaution to ask – politely of course – which other agent, if any, sold the property and who purchased it.

This is where your accurate record keeping comes to the fore. If the seller claims a private sale, and you gave the particulars of his property to the buyer, then you could have a claim for commission, provided you can prove that you introduced the buyer to the property *before* the seller did.

You could even claim some of the credit for the sale, if the buyer called into the property having seen your For Sale board outside.

Unfortunately, this is something of a grey area and one agents try to avoid at all costs. Should you find yourself in such a position, however, and think you have a valid claim for your commission, make sure all your records verify the claim. In many cases, an amicable arrangement can be made with the seller, perhaps by negotiating a slightly reduced commission due to the fact that you did not escort the buyer to the property in the first place. Such an arrangement will of course depend upon the circumstances.

If you lost the sale to another agent, then it is probably your own fault anyway. Perhaps you did not project the right image, or show enough interest, or simply did not evaluate the needs of your applicant correctly.

Another reason for not divulging the addresses of properties, unless applicants are willing to leave their name and address, is that of security. In today's unsettled climate, you can never be too careful!

Never assume that an enquiry is from a time-waster – someone with no intention of buying or selling anything at all. That person may not intend to move right away, but the very fact that he has bothered to contact you shows he has at least a basic interest in property.

Many agents only retain names and addresses on mailing lists for a few weeks and then discard them. The enterprising agent, however, will not take an applicant off his list until he has established that the applicant is definitely suited.

He will telephone the applicant as soon as a suitable property is registered. He will also follow up mail-shots with a telephone call to find out if any of the details sent were of interest and to make viewing arrangements.

From this contact the agent will establish a good rapport with the applicant and will find it easy to make viewing arrangements which may soon produce a sale. He can also arrange to value the applicant's property, where appropriate, so ensuring that no potential sale or instruction to sell is overlooked or lost to a competitor, at the same time keeping mailing lists well up to date.

Providing information

The good salesman will make sure that customers are fully aware of *all* the services he is able to offer. The estate agent is no exception.

Brochures and leaflets are one way of telling customers that you can arrange mortgages, carry out valuations, give financial advice, act as an agent for a building society, and so on, but by talking to people, and putting those services into practice, you will encourage far more business and soon build up a reputation for providing help and advice when and where it is needed.

Maps of the area are useful, too, even to those customers already familiar with the area.

Your specifications are, however, more important. They must be accurate, perfectly presented with a colour photograph if possible, and should reflect your care and attention to detail. (See Chapter 3 for more about specifications.) The appeal – or lack of it – of your specification projects much of your business image. Often, too, it is your main outlet for providing information about the properties on your register.

If possible, present the details of properties, together with a map and further information about the services you offer, in a matching folder.

The personal touch

An attentive agent will spend time with his applicant, going through particulars of properties and pointing out specific details about each. He will listen carefully to comments made by the customer, from which he will soon determine exactly what type of property that customer will eventually buy, and also secure the customer's instruction to act as his selling agent if this is appropriate.

But in order to talk with any authority to your customer, it is imperative that you have sound product knowledge. Your customers will not be impressed if you are unable to tell them anything more about a property than is in your specification. They need to be persuaded to view. They need to know some of those special details which are not necessarily written down – perhaps the colour scheme of the interior, or the amount of wear and tear showing on the fitted carpets that are being included in the price.

You must also know your area and understand how the location of a property will affect its price and resale value. All property is affected by the area in which it is located, or the level of employment in that area. If unemployment is high, and people are unlikely to be moving into the area, then prices will remain stagnant or begin to drop. People anxious to move to locations where they may find a job then find themselves having to sell at a much lower figure than they anticipated – if they can sell at all.

At the other end of the scale, property in the heart of busy cities and towns is always in demand and can command very high prices indeed.

The general buoyancy of the market also affects prices, for instance the availability of mortgages, or when demand is high and there are few properties available.

If you can demonstrate your knowledge of the market, and show a personal interest in your customer's needs, you will not find it difficult to persuade people to view, but if you show lack of interest coupled with lack of product knowledge, you are unlikely to persuade anyone to look at anything at all.

Making viewing arrangements

Having decided the type of property your customer is looking for, you should take care to give him the details of every property that is likely to be of interest. If you miss one out, that will undoubtedly be the one your customer will be taken to see by another agent. As we have said, commission is due to the agent who first introduces the buyer to the property. Make sure it's you.

Make viewing arrangements while the customer is with you. Write the name of the seller and the time of the appointment at the top of each specification so there can be no query. Wherever possible, take the customer to view the property yourself.

Escorted viewings are usually the most successful. Either take the customer in your own car or meet him at the property. Only make arrangements for the viewer to visit the property on his own if there really is no alternative.

Many sellers much prefer their agent to show viewers around their property anyway, and for people living on their own, or perhaps the elderly or infirm it is, of course, a matter of common sense and courtesy to take the customer yourself.

You can learn a great deal about your customer's special likes and dislikes by taking him yourself, and you can direct his interest elsewhere if it is obvious this is not the property for him. It is not always easy to persuade someone that the type of property they are asking for is probably not the best one they could buy, but better to do it now than to negotiate a sale and then find the purchaser changes his mind, or is refused a suitable mortgage.

Follow up every viewing promptly, and report back to the seller immediately, even if the viewer did not like the property at all. In fact, it often helps to tell the seller exactly what the viewer didn't like and why he doesn't want to buy. It builds up a picture of the saleability of the property and establishes whether or not its price reflects the sort of value buyers are expecting for their money.

When you follow up a viewing you may even find that the customer liked the property but did not think he could afford it and therefore did not bother to come back to you. He may be pleasantly surprised if you are able to negotiate an acceptable offer and thus secure a sale.

Key systems

Because on-the-spot viewing arrangements are often demanded, and because sellers may be at work all day, or the property is vacant, it is sometimes necessary to hold the key of the property to take people to view.

A secure key system is imperative. There are many ways of keeping keys safely, but the following points should be observed:

- Never label the key with the address in case of loss. A number is more suitable and can be cross-referenced with a central register or key-book.
- Keep all keys in a secure place, away from your main office.
- Every time a key is taken out by a member of staff, it should be signed out and signed back into the system after use. The date and the time the key was taken should also be recorded. The key-book itself should be used for this purpose.
- *Never* hand a key to a customer and allow him to view the property without you – even if the property is vacant.
- Even the seller must sign for the key if he takes it out of your office.
- You cannot release a key to a buyer unless you check with the seller's solicitor that legal completion has taken place and all the money has been received for the property in exchange for the keys. You will sometimes find buyers calling in to collect keys with their removal van outside, but you must still not release the key unless you get authority to do so from the seller's solicitor, and this could mean keeping the buyer waiting for several hours until the legal formalities are completed. Receipt of the key must still be verified by the buyer's signature.

If the seller is still in residence, you must contact him before taking people to view. Don't just walk in and expect it to be convenient. Having a key does not give you free access to your client's property. If the seller is not at home, leave your business card somewhere in the house to acknowledge that you have been there, and make sure you leave the property securely locked up after you leave.

If the property is empty, check that windows and doors are secure and that the property has not been vandalised or broken into. If the weather is extremely severe, make sure water tanks, central heating systems and so on are not frozen or damaged in any way. If you spot any potential problem, report it immediately to the seller and, if necessary, arrange to have remedial work carried out.

Most building society surveyors do not expect agents to accompany them while they carry out a survey. However, do not release the keys of a property to a surveyor without first getting authority from the seller, and, of course, ensuring the key is signed for in the usual way.

Making the sale

Your customer's reaction to a particular property will immediately reflect his like or dislike of it. If you take a customer to view a property, he is more likely to tell you immediately whether or not he wishes to buy it. If you have arranged for him to view on his own, however, you will probably have an anxious vendor on the telephone informing you that the customer promised he would 'let the agent know'. The problem here, of course, is that most people say they will 'be in touch with the agent' when they have no intention of doing so at all – another reason for effective follow-up procedures.

If several agents have the same property on their registers, then in order to secure a sale, you must move quickly. As soon as the property is registered with you, telephone applicants on your register who are in a strong position to proceed. This is where your 'hot list' is so useful. The whole idea is to be the first agent to introduce a buyer to the property. All those applicants you have on your register are likely to be on other agents' registers too. You need to be the first agent to make the contact and arrange the viewing if you are to secure the sale.

Make sure you either take the applicant to, or meet him at, the property. If you don't, another agent will.

The right buyer for the right house

Many people wish to buy property but cannot do so until their own property is sold. The question then arises, should they sell first or buy first? This will depend a great deal on the circumstances involved, but if the people involved are dependent upon the sale of one property before another purchase can be made, and they are determined to move anyway, then they should put their property on the market as soon as possible.

As their agent, it will then be up to you to make sure you introduce a buyer to the property who can fall in line with any time constraints which may apply. If, for instance, the vendor has still not found a property to buy, you must make this clear to prospective buyers and make sure they are in a position to wait.

On the other hand, many people prefer to find a property to buy before they put their own on the market, in which case you will need to find a purchaser who can proceed fairly quickly, preferably without another property to sell, or with a property which is already sold subject to contract. What you need to avoid is a long chain of uncompleted transactions. Of course, these can never be avoided entirely – such is the structure of the property market in general – but you will only be acting in the best interests of your client if you endeavour to find a purchaser who is in the strongest possible position to complete the transaction.

Don't agree a sale unless you have reason to believe that you have found the right person for the right property, one who can meet all the constraints involved. You need to check:

(a) that he can obtain a suitable mortgage if one is required
(b) that the advance will be forthcoming in time
(c) that he has sold his own property subject to contract, or is about to do so
(d) if he has not sold, that he can obtain suitable bridging finance, or
(e) that he is a first-time buyer with nothing to sell anyway, or
(f) that he is a cash buyer.

Let us look more closely at each of these elements.

(a) Your buyer may have already arranged a mortgage in principle. Some lenders now confirm this arrangement in writing to assure agents and sellers that they agree to make a loan, subject to survey. Take the precaution, however, of checking what percentage of advance the buyer requires. Bear in mind that lenders expect to find a property in good order before they are prepared to make a high advance. Certain other factors will also be taken into account, such as the age of the property, whether it has a sitting tenant, whether it is leasehold or freehold, and so on (see Chapter 4 for further details).

(b) If the seller needs to complete the transaction within certain time limits, and if the mortgage is required at a time when long queues of borrowers are in evidence, then it is possible that the loan will not be forthcoming in time. If there is some doubt as to whether or not a suitable advance will be obtained, then your own mortgage sources should be investigated. If you act for a building society, then they should treat any application from you as a priority. This could well mean the difference between your customer obtaining a mortgage right away, or having to wait at the end of a queue for several months. So if there is a problem, or if your customer has not yet applied for a mortgage, then your own sources should be approached.

(c) Chains of sales and purchases can appear never-ending unless

contracts have been exchanged, so you need to find out from your purchaser how far his sale has progressed. Take the name and address of his selling agent and solicitor so that you can check on the current position. Don't take the purchaser's word that he has exchanged contracts unless this is also checked out. Very often solicitors call in their clients to sign contracts and pay their deposit, and then hold on to the contract while last-minute problems are sorted out. Even then, chains of sales can still break down, and exchange does not take place.
(d) Although your buyer may have a property to sell, he could be in a position to obtain bridging finance in order to complete the transaction. Here, again, it is advisable to verify that bridging has been arranged via your customer's solicitor. In the best interests of your client, you cannot rely on a prospective buyer just 'hoping' he can raise the money!
(e) First-time buyers are much easier to deal with, provided any mortgage they require can be obtained. Many first-time buyers do not fully understand what is involved in obtaining a mortgage, and here your attention and advice will be needed, as well as your knowledge and understanding of mortgage procedures. Many lenders offer special mortgage packages for first-time buyers and these are discussed in more detail in Chapter 4.
(f) Your customer could be in a position to pay cash – pay for the property from his own resources – in order to complete the transaction. Here the worry of obtaining suitable financing is alleviated, but beware the customer who tells you he will pay cash and omits to explain that such cash can only be raised if he sells his existing property. Here, again, a telephone call to the customer's solicitor to confirm details is required.

If you are acting as agent for everyone involved in a chain of sales and purchases, this will put you in a prime position to monitor progress and to ensure that a satisfactory completion is reached. However, in practice, this is most unlikely. At best you can expect to act for perhaps two people involved in the same chain, and it then falls upon you to keep in close contact with other selling agents and solicitors in order to check on progress as the transaction proceeds.

A sale should only be agreed with the buyer who is in the strongest possible position to proceed with, and eventually complete, the transaction. If there is some doubt, then offer first refusal until the buyer's position improves, or unless a more suitable purchaser is found. In this way, you keep your options open while at the same time you take the most suitable course of action for your client.

Contract races

It is not a good idea to involve buyers in contract races. Having said that, however, it could be in the best interests of your client, especially when tight time factors are involved.

The client himself is perfectly entitled to give instructions that a contract should be issued to more than one buyer, and the first person to sign and exchange the contract will win the race.

Avoid the situation where your own customers are involved in a race for the same property. But where a buyer from another agency could well win the day, it is worth doing all in your power to secure exchange of contracts as soon as possible in favour of your own customer. In such a case it is imperative that you push through the transaction at every level, arranging mortgages and surveys, pestering solicitors and, if necessary, acting as courier in order to ensure that documents reach their destination as quickly as possible.

You must make it clear to your customer that he is involved in a contract race, and that should he lose, survey fees and any other legal costs incurred will still have to be paid. However, it is worth mentioning that if a mortgage has been arranged and the sale falls through, the lender will usually hold the application for a certain length of time (usually indicated on the mortgage offer) and, subject to survey, the allocated amount of the loan can be transferred to another property.

Putting forward offers

As soon as you receive an offer for a property, you are legally obliged to put it forward to the seller – whatever it is. Even if a sale is already progressing towards exchange of contracts, should another offer be forthcoming it must be put forward to the seller. Find out all you can about a prospective buyer in order to keep your seller properly informed. Make your views known too. If you do not consider the buyer to be reliable, then say so, and suggest to your client that he is given first refusal at this stage, but that no firm arrangement is entered into until his position improves.

If you have been instructed to accept offers *above* a certain level, then each offer must be considered on its merit, taking into account the purchasing capability of the buyer as already discussed.

It is not a good idea to contact the seller and put forward an offer in front of the buyer. You may need to tell the seller that you don't think the offer is good enough, and discuss other offers received or which might be received – the sort of conversation the prospective buyer should not overhear. You must understand at this crucial point that if there is a conflict of interests, you represent the seller *not* the buyer, and any decisions made must be to the advantage of the seller regardless of your feelings towards the buyer. If the offer is too low, you will need to barter until a mutually acceptable figure is reached.

If you think the offer is sound, the buyer is in a strong position to proceed and there is a good chance of him getting the mortgage he requires – and you have checked all this out – make sure the seller is fully aware of the position. If he is considering an offer from another agent, he needs to be persuaded to accept the offer from *your* customer. Make sure he does.

A property is deemed to be *under offer* or *sold subject to contract* after an offer has been agreed and accepted and the legal formalities are under way, but prior to exchange of contracts. Some agents will take a property off the market at this stage, but most will continue to offer it, though at a lower profile, in order to line up a second buyer in case the first sale should fall through for any reason. As long as all parties are fully aware of the situation, it is certainly worth keeping your options open until contracts are exchanged, but make it clear to the secondary buyer that he can only go ahead if the first sale falls through.

Confirming the details

Once an offer has been agreed and accepted, complete your pro forma and send a copy to the buyer's solicitor and the seller's solicitor, together with a copy of your specification. Your pro forma will contain all the information they need.

Suggested format for letter to seller's solicitor

> Re: (full address of property)
>
> We are pleased to confirm that we have agreed the sale of the above property on behalf of our mutual client (seller's full name) at the agreed and accepted price of £00000 subject to contract and survey as per the attached pro forma, and we would ask you to issue draft contracts to the purchaser's solicitor as soon as possible.
>
> If you require any further information or assistance please do not hesitate to contact us.

You should also ask the buyer to keep you informed of his progress with mortgage arrangements and, of course, arrangements for any surveys he requires. If, at any time, there is a change to the agreed and accepted purchase price of the property, this must be confirmed in writing to the seller and his solicitor and to the buyer and his solicitor. The buyer must

Suggested format for letter to buyer's solicitor

> Re: (full address of property)
>
> We are pleased to confirm that we have agreed the sale of the above property to your client (buyer's name) at the agreed and accepted price of £00000 subject to contract and survey as per the attached pro forma.
>
> We have today written to (name of seller's solicitor) requesting them to forward a draft contract to you as soon as possible.
>
> If you require any further information or assistance, please do not hesitate to contact us.

It is also necessary to confirm the details of the sale to both the buyer and the seller.

Suggested format for letter to seller

> Re: (full address of property)
>
> We are pleased to confirm that our applicant (name of buyer) has agreed to purchase the above property for the sum of £00000 subject to contract and survey, and that his offer to purchase at that price has been agreed and accepted by you.
>
> We have today instructed your solicitor to issue draft contracts to (name of buyer)'s solicitor and we will keep you fully informed of the progress of the transaction.

Many agents like to reaffirm the details of their commission arrangements in their confirmation of sale letter, and you should end the letter by politely offering any further help or assistance the seller may need.

Suggested format for letter to buyer

> Re: (full address of property)
>
> We are pleased to confirm that your offer of £00000 subject to contract and survey for the above property has been agreed and accepted by our client.
>
> We have today instructed our client's solicitor (name and address of seller's solicitor) to issue draft contracts to (name of buyer's solicitor), whom we understand are to act on your behalf, and we trust that a speedy and satisfactory completion will be reached.

also inform his building society of the change, especially if it is going to affect the amount of advance. Should the deal be cancelled, then this too must be confirmed in writing to all concerned.

Most agents devise a range of standard letters which they use. If you have a typewriter with a memory function, or a word processor on which such letters can be stored, you will save a great deal of time and effort and the wording will always be correct. Your only task is to insert names and addresses as appropriate.

You may wish to devise standard letters to fit the following categories:

- confirmation of sale letter to seller
- confirmation of sale letter to buyer
- confirmation of sale letter to seller's solicitor
- confirmation of sale letter to buyer's solicitor
- letters to each of the above when a sale is cancelled
- confirmation of instruction to sell to seller
- letter to other agent(s) instructing them to act as sub-agents
- letter to other agent(s) confirming their instruction to you to act as their sub-agent
- letter to seller confirming a price change
- letter to seller's solicitor enclosing your invoice after exchange of contracts has taken place
- letter to seller's solicitor acknowledging receipt of your commission cheque.

Dealing with fixtures and fittings

A fixture is deemed to be an item fixed to, or built into, the property in such a way that to remove it would cause damage to the property itself. However, it is argued that items such as bathroom fittings can easily be removed and walls or decor reinstated leaving no evidence of their demise. The matter of fixtures and fittings in a property can therefore pose a problem and, as a selling agent, take care to ensure that you do not include in your specification of the property any fixtures and fittings that the seller does not intend to leave.

Where the seller intends to include items such as carpets, curtains or other fixtures and fittings in the asking price, and there is absolutely no doubt that these *will* be left, you can mention them on your specification. If in doubt, leave them out.

In some cases carpets and curtains can be a point of negotiation. If a low offer is made to the seller, he might accept it on condition that the carpets and curtains mentioned on the specification are no longer to be included. If this happens, make sure the arrangement is mentioned in your letters confirming the sale.

It should also be noted that, for the purpose of a building society survey it is the value of the property itself which is being assessed and not the fixtures and fittings left in it.

Handling deposits

Under the Estate Agents Act 1979, it becomes a criminal offence to take a deposit unless you have insurance to cover the loss of clients' money.

Agents who are bonded members of the National Association of Estate Agents have cover for their clients, offering assurance that should any money go astray, appropriate steps will be taken by the Association to recover the loss, but *all* agents should have proper insurance cover.

You must have a special bank account for this purpose and any deposits paid must be kept there and not in your own account. However, if you earn interest on the account, you can usually keep it for yourself.

Prospective purchasers are not legally obliged to pay a deposit, and you cannot force them to do so, but if you accept a deposit, you must ensure that a proper receipt is issued. If the sale does not materialise, then you must return the deposit in full.

The law only makes a special clients' account compulsory if the property is being sold in the United Kingdom. It does not apply to property abroad.

Making sure completion is reached

Although you have in fact met your obligation to your client by introducing a purchaser to his property, it is by no means the end of the road. If you are to secure the sale and make sure it reaches completion, you must monitor it closely and be ready to take remedial action as soon as problems arise.

This means keeping in close contact with the buyer, checking that his mortgage arrangements are running smoothly, making sure a surveyor has arrived, finding out when the mortgage offer itself has been received, and, of course, keeping in touch with solicitors in order to ensure there is no hold-up or problems with the legal proceedings.

If other agents are involved in a chain of sales and purchases beyond your own transaction, keep in close contact with them to make sure their link in the chain continues to make progress. It is the lack of constant and informative liaison which often leads to the break-down of chains, usually resulting in the estate agent being blamed, whether or not he had any control over the matter.

You may find it necessary to take the drastic step of putting the property back on the open market – although you should have a second buyer lined up anyway. You may also have to sort out problems with the buyer's mortgage. You will soon learn how different lenders treat different situations, and you may find it necessary to place a mortgage with a different lender in order to ensure that a more suitable advance is forthcoming.

Often, buyers and sellers do not fully understand what is going on. They misinterpret messages, or simply fail to keep the agent, solicitors, surveyors or even lenders fully informed as to what action they have taken and why. Unfortunately, this can lead to a great deal of confusion and bad feeling among all those concerned, and it may well fall to you as the selling agent to sort out all the difficulties and calm everyone down. This is when your counselling skills and patience are most needed, for if complaints are to be made, they will undoubtedly be made to you. It is at times like these that the agent who monitors his sales efficiently, and takes all the steps necessary to ensure that completion is reached, will succeed in his efforts where other, less attentive agents will fail.

Gazumping

Once a sale has been agreed and is under way, it is assumed that a gentleman's agreement loosely binds the seller to staying with the same buyer until exchange of contracts. However, there is no reason why the seller should not accept a higher offer for his property at any time prior to legal exchange, and as his agent, you are certainly obliged to put forward any offers which you receive. The final decision then lies with the seller as to which offer he will accept.

If a higher offer is received after a sale has been agreed, it is usually accepted by the seller, and although buyers who have been gazumped in this way are bound to be disappointed, especially if they have already paid survey fees and so on, unfortunately there is absolutely nothing they can do about it.

If you find your client has accepted a higher offer via another agent, however, there are certain steps you should take to save your original sale, the most important being to ascertain what the new offer is, and to persuade the seller to give *your* buyer the opportunity to raise his bid to meet the new one. If the sale has been under way for some time, then this is obviously the best course of action from everyone's point of view, as the legal paperwork will already have been drawn up. What you must do then is to persuade the buyer that all is not lost.

Most lenders understand the problems, and even if mortgage arrangements are complete, they may well consider advancing an additional amount to meet the difference. A telephone call may be all that is necessary to make such arrangements, and if your buyer is in agreement, it may be just enough to clinch the sale.

If the buyer is unable to meet the higher offer in full, you could perhaps make some arrangement with regard to your commission so that some of the difference is made up by you reducing your fee to the seller, leaving the buyer to find only some of the outstanding amount.

The final option could be to persuade the seller to turn the whole thing into a contract race. This sometimes proves successful if the seller is committed to completing the sale within certain time limits. If the transaction you originally negotiated has already made good progress, then you could well win the race and save the sale. Whatever happens, don't give up on your sale!

Early in 1987 steps were taken to curb the increase in gazumping, and a report was published on behalf of the Law Commission suggesting that both buyer and seller pay a voluntary deposit of 0.5 per cent when a sale is agreed. Later, another suggestion was put forward that each party be *bound* to pay the deposit which would be forfeited if contracts were not exchanged within four weeks without good reason. However, this is still a matter for discussion and it remains to be seen what will come of it.

Down-valuations

A surveyor acting on behalf of a lender has to ascertain that the property is adequate security for the loan applied for. He needs to make sure that if the buyer fails to meet the repayments on the advance, the lender can sell the property and get his money back, including all the costs incurred. The lender will base his offer of an advance on this valuation, the maximum amount of the advance being 75 or 80 per cent of the valuation figure and not the asking price.

If the surveyor does not consider that the resale value of the property will cover the amount of the advance applied for, he will down-value the property and the amount offered will be reduced accordingly.

Retentions

The surveyor will also expect the property to be of a certain standard. If it is not, then he will recommend that a certain amount of the advance be retained by the lender until work has been carried out which brings the property up to the standard required. An itemised list of the work will be provided, and the amount of the retention should be in line with the estimated cost of having the work carried out.

If the buyer decides to continue with the purchase and has no extra cash readily available, he may need to obtain bridging finance from his bank in order to make up the deficit caused by the retention. He will then have to arrange for the work to be carried out and, on completion of the work, pay another inspection fee to the lender. This second fee is slightly less than the original amount paid, and on receipt of this, the surveyor will once again visit the property to inspect the work and make sure it is up to the standard he requires. If it is, the amount of money retained will be released. A retention could also be made on a new property until the local authority takes over the roads and access ways.

In cases of down-valuations and retentions, if the differential between amounts is limited, a sale can possibly be saved by negotiating a reduction in the purchase price to cover the amount, or at least part of it. Alternatively, you could reduce your commission to the seller so that he can lower the asking price and help the buyer to balance his finances in order to complete the purchase.

Conclusion

The secret of selling property is to establish exactly what your customers are looking for, remembering that although they may have a type of property in mind, the chances are it will not be the type of property they eventually buy.

You must also take into account their mortgage requirements and make sure you don't sell them a property which is unlikely to be approved as suitable security by the lender.

If you take people to view, you will find it much easier to assess their response and identify their likes and dislikes. You will see, too, their reaction when a property *feels* right for them. This is not something you can explain or describe to anyone, but there is a certain something that people feel when they find that special property which is right for them – and that is the property they will want to buy, even if it is not at all what they first set out to purchase.

Don't accept the loss of a sale at face value. If you have monitored the sale properly, then you should have taken the necessary steps to save it. If you haven't, however, don't give up. Explore every avenue open to you. Use your skills as a salesman and adviser to keep your sale intact.

Assignment 2: Viewing analysis

Objective

- To assess the value of effective viewing arrangements

Tasks

1. From your records for the last three months, provide a break-down analysis for:
   (a) the number of viewings in all
   (b) the number of escorted viewings
   (c) the number of viewings arranged after following up mail-shots
2. Determine the number of sales achieved from:
   (a) escorted viewings
   (b) unescorted viewings
3. Report on your findings.
4. Identify any viewing arrangements that were not carried out efficiently, or not recorded exactly. Ascertain why this was and what problems arose because of it.
5. Recommend any action you consider necessary to improve your viewing system.

Assignment 3: Problem solving

Objectives

- To analyse difficulties and problems which have arisen resulting in the loss of a sale
- To establish what steps could have been taken in order to save the sale
- To look at your follow-up techniques and identify weaknesses

Tasks

1. From your records of sales which have not completed, identify the problems which arose and the reason why the sale was not successful.
2. If another agent made the sale, establish why he was successful and you were not.
3. Identify the point where the sale fell through, and from your records, establish what follow-up procedures were taken at that point.
4. List the steps which could have been taken to prevent the sale you have analysed from falling through.
5. Write a report outlining how your follow-up techniques can be improved to ensure that the same problems can be avoided in the future.

6. Look at all your follow-up procedures and identify any areas where they could be improved in order to create more viewing arrangements, valuations, instructions, or to monitor ongoing sales more efficiently.

Chapter 3

Building Up Your Register

Introduction

You cannot sell houses unless you have received instructions from sellers to act on their behalf.

Building up a register of properties, however, is not always as easy as it may seem and the number of properties on your register at any one time can vary considerably. There are often quiet times, such as Christmas and New Year, and when mortgages are easily obtainable, supply does not always meet demand, whereas a mortgage famine can create a backlog of unsold properties.

To encourage sellers to instruct you when you first open your agency, you could offer a specially reduced introductory commission. This encourages business and promotes business growth by giving you the opportunity of proving your worth, so building up your register by recommendation and making your presence felt in the area.

In this chapter we will be looking at the process of obtaining instructions to sell, carrying out valuations and preparing specifications in order to build up a register of properties ready to sell.

Getting off the ground

There are many ways of establishing your own identity in the area where you intend to open your business. 'Opening Soon' stickers on your window will encourage enquiries even before the premises are quite ready, and a leaflet drop in the area offering a specially reduced commission rate for a limited period would also be helpful. There are many organisations which provide a leaflet distribution service, and charges are based on the number of leaflets dropped and the area to be covered. Another source is to have your leaflets distributed inside local papers which also contain back-up advertising material.

Take advantage of as many advertising outlets as are available to you, and include details of all the other services you can offer. Use your local radio station, too, and as soon as you receive instructions, advertise each property immediately in order to make sales as soon as possible and to build up your mailing list.

Turning enquiries into instructions

The importance of effective follow-up techniques comes to the fore again. Many of the applicants on your mailing list will live in your area and, before they can buy a property, they will have to sell their own. When you follow up enquiries and mail-shots, take the opportunity of offering to carry out a free market valuation for those applicants. Suggest that until the applicant knows the selling value of his existing home, he will find it difficult to determine the top price he will be able to afford for a new one. Very few agents charge a fee for this service, so emphasise this – it's free and is the most sensible course of action open to the applicant at this stage of his house-hunting.

Emphasise all the other services you offer too, such as arranging mortgages for prospective buyers, and how you pay special attention to following up sales in order to make sure each one reaches a satisfactory completion. If you are able to arrange surveys or help with insurance matters, then let your applicant know. Convince him that your advertising and working methods are the most appropriate for his needs, and the personal attention you will give to the sale of his property is unlikely to be bettered by anyone else.

It is, of course, just as important to tackle the personal caller in much the same way. If you can convince him of the necessity to have a market valuation, you immediately open the door to an instruction.

Don't wait until the applicant finds a property he wants to buy. If he buys from another agent, then that agent will inevitably receive his instruction to sell. You need to convince the applicant that he should put his property on the market as soon as possible or he will not be in a strong position to enter into negotiations to buy.

If you can arrange a valuation at this very early stage, you can take the instruction under a sole agency agreement, thus eliminating your competitors from that property.

There is always the problem, however, of the applicant who has already instructed another agent. If a sole agency has been agreed then you need to point out that the applicant can instruct as many agents as he chooses, and if the agreement has been running for some time, why hasn't his property been sold? Here you should determine the time limit imposed on the sole agency instruction, and suggest that you act as selling agent when the term has expired.

The success of your tactics will depend largely on the circumstances of each applicant, but with the right approach the applicant can be made to understand the importance of having a valuation carried out and why he should instruct *you* to act on his behalf. If a seller approaches you with the intention of giving you the instruction anyway, it is a much easier situation to deal with, and if you are the first agent instructed, a sole agency agreement will again eliminate other agents from that property.

Touting – the dangers

Touting can take many forms. It is in fact poaching properties which are already for sale, perhaps by knocking on doors where there is another agent's board outside or dropping letters asking for business through letter-boxes. Some agents also obtain other agents' particulars in various ways, not only to keep an eye on competition, but also to establish contact with the seller. Following up private advertisements and asking for instructions is yet another form of touting.

The National Association of Estate Agents does not approve of touting and it is fair to say that most sellers also disapprove. They object to being pestered for business, and although it cannot be denied that touting goes on in various forms, it is certainly not something which is readily accepted nor does it do anything to improve the image of the profession.

Valuations

Not all negotiators are professional, qualified surveyors and members of the Royal Institution of Chartered Surveyors or the Incorporated Society of Valuers and Auctioneers, but this does not prevent them from carrying out valuations for the purpose of establishing a realistic marketing price for a property.

However, sound product knowledge is essential, as is an in-depth appreciation and awareness of the current selling prices of similar property in the same vicinity. This is not an area where you can afford to make errors. Your credibility as a knowledgeable and professional agent can be lost at a stroke if you miscalculate, and you could even find yourself being sued if matters get out of hand.

Let us look in more detail at the process of carrying out a valuation and what is involved.

The general buoyancy of the market

This means the level of enquiries being received, the availability of mortgage funds and any seasonal factors which could contribute to the current position of the market as a whole.

Comparing prices of other similar properties

You must know what other properties are currently for sale, what competition they offer in terms of value for money, and what price they are being marketed for.

Knowing the area well

You will soon appreciate how different locations within your area command different values, even for houses which are very similar. You will probably find too that you receive more enquiries for one area than for another even though the properties are virtually the same in both. There are certain factors which also affect the saleability of the property, for example:

- its proximity to a public house, or night-club, or even a fast-food take-away store where it could be noisy and there could be problems with parking
- whether there are any plans for extensive development in the immediate area
- if there is an industrial complex nearby
- if the property backs on to fields or a wooded area it could be more desirable
- if it is situated within easy access to motorways or train stations for those who commute to work
- if there is employment in the area then this will certainly affect demand.

You may be asked to value a listed building which is of architectural or historic value. Here the owner cannot change the appearance of the property without first seeking the appropriate planning consent, although it is often possible to obtain a grant to improve and maintain the property if it falls below a certain standard. Such properties often fall into conservation areas where the same rules apply. If you want to find out more about the listed buildings in your own area, check with your local authority.

Age, construction and general condition of the property

This is also a crucial point, bearing in mind the restrictions lenders might apply to advances on property which is not brick under tile, or property which was built before a certain year.

Although you will not be carrying out a survey as such, there are several things you need to look out for which could affect the mortgageability of the property and your final valuation figure. These include:

Outside

Go to the end of the garden and take a good look at the outside of the property. Check for missing roof tiles or chimney stacks which need attention. If there is a flat roof, ask the seller when it was laid and if any guarantees currently apply.

Make sure the walls are straight with no obvious cracks or bulges (could be caused by settlement).

Make sure repointing is not necessary.

Check the damp-proof course. Is it exposed all around the property or are there signs of damp at that level? If the cavity between the inner and outer walls is full of debris causing dampness, it is an expensive problem to be rectified.

Also look at downpipes and guttering and check that they too are in good condition and not blocked or damaged, causing damp and water penetration.

Take details of any sheds, summer-houses or other outbuildings included in the sale, together with a description of the garden and plot size.

Inside

Again check for evidence of damp, especially in bathrooms and kitchens where silverfish may lurk in wet areas. Inspect internal walls for tide marks, yellowing or mould – further signs of rising damp or worse.

Walls should be straight and level and door and window frames correctly aligned, each opening and closing snugly into position. Cracks in walls or doors out of true could also be due to settlement.

There should be no evidence of dampness or severe cracking at ceiling level.

Check condition of sanitaryware and kitchen fittings. Any built-in appliances should be clean and in good working order.

Central heating systems should also be in good working order and, where appropriate, serviced regularly. If oil-fired central heating is installed, ask how much oil is currently stored and likely to be included with the sale.

If rewiring has been carried out, check that this was done by a professional electrician. Ask if there are guarantees.

Bear in mind that most do-it-yourself enthusiasts do a fairly good job, but not all.

If the property has been extended, check that planning consent was obtained.

All woodwork must be in a good state of repair. Timber treatment does not come cheap. Where this has already been carried out, guarantees should be available.

There should also be guarantees for any new windows or double glazing installed.

Make sure there is adequate insulation. If cavity wall insulation has been installed, check what type and make sure there is a guarantee.

The mortgageability of the property

This is another essential point to consider. You will need to make sure that you introduce a buyer who can complete the purchase. If that buyer requires a high mortgage in relation to the asking price, and the property is unlikely to be valued at that price, then it will be no good negotiating a sale to him. A lender will be reluctant to offer a high advance on:

- a property of unconventional construction
- a leasehold property with only a few years remaining on the lease
- a flat or maisonette above a certain number of floors (usually about four)
- a flat above a shop
- a property which fronts directly on to the street
- a property built before a certain date
- a property with a sitting tenant
- a property without inside toilet and bathroom facilities
- a converted flat rather than a purpose-built one. (This ruling is often relaxed in London where many properties have been converted into flats rather than being purpose built.)

Each lender will have his own rules and regulations regarding these points, and it is up to you to find out what they are from the lender or lenders you will be associated with.

Home improvement grants

It could be possible for the buyer to obtain a grant towards improving the home he buys, and if this is likely, it could affect your value of the property.

Some properties are certainly eligible for home improvement grants, especially if they do not have adequate bathroom or toilet facilities. The amount of grant will depend on what the local authority deem to be an 'eligible expense'. This includes:

- the installation of internal bathroom facilities incorporating bath or shower, wash hand basin, wc
- hot and cold water supply to the above.

The amount received will be a proportion of the total expense and other grants will be at the discretion of the local authority. In Greater London the amounts are usually slightly higher than elsewhere in the country. A leaflet called 'Home Improvement Grants – A Guide for Homeowners, Landlords and Tenants', can be obtained from your local authority.

Terms and conditions of leasehold property

The value of a leasehold property is also affected by the terms and conditions of the lease, together with the number of years left outstanding on the lease. A lease with only a few years left to run will greatly reduce the current value of the property, as at the end of the term the lease reverts to the freeholder. Find out as much as you can about any lease that applies to the property before you decide on your final valuation figure.

Finally, bear in mind at all times that if you over-value – as some agents do in order to secure the instruction – the chances are that the property will remain on the market for a long period and, even if you do find a buyer, a down-valuation is likely and you will then have a very annoyed vendor to contend with. If you under-value, however, it can be a potentially more serious situation. You will undoubtedly sell the property, but you could find yourself involved in a law suit demanding compensation for the difference between your valuation and the true value of the property, plus all the expenses incurred by the vendor through your inefficiency.

Often a vendor will expect you to market his property for a higher price than you come up with. Of course, this is entirely up to him, and as his agent you must act on his instruction, but it is a wise precaution to make your feelings about the price perfectly clear right from the start. You will market the property at the figure he chooses, but monitor response carefully and keep in touch with the seller so that if there is no interest shown, you can, perhaps after an agreed trial period, reduce the asking price. Very often sellers learn from their own mistakes. They will soon realise the problem when no one arrives to view, but make sure you keep in touch with the seller throughout the trial period or he will assume no one has called due to your inefficiency and not due to the fact that the property is overpriced.

If there are other factors which influence the number of people viewing, such as lack of mortgage funds, lack of demand for property in that particular area or a general slump in the market, then you must still keep in contact with the seller and make him fully aware of the situation so that he realises you are doing your best and he has not been forgotten. Keeping in regular contact with sellers is essential, whether or not there are people viewing.

Putting the property to auction

If the property is of unusual construction, or is difficult to value accurately, you may suggest that in the interest of the seller, it is put up for auction. This is often appropriate when properties are unlikely to be mortgageable, if there is a sitting tenant, or perhaps if a trustee is arranging the sale and has to show that the highest possible price for the property has been obtained.

Arrangements for auctions can be made through a member of the Incorporated Society of Valuers and Auctioneers. Fees are usually negotiable and will depend on the arrangement made with the client. This could be a sole selling right where even if the seller sells the property privately, his agent must be paid the agreed fee. Some agents also charge for advertising, plus the cost of the auction, whether or not the property is sold. In conjunction with the auctioneer, you will need to draw up a specification of the property in great detail, including any special terms and conditions of sale outlined by the seller or his solicitor. This should be in line with the Law Society's *General Conditions of Sale*, a copy of which should be available on request.

If a reserve price is set on the property, this must not be revealed to prospective buyers, and sales particulars should state 'subject to reserve price'. Your client can also retain the option to accept offers prior to the date of the auction, in which case you need to state 'unless previously sold by private treaty'.

Prior to the auction any interested buyer will need to have an independent survey carried out and be in a position to raise the capital on or before the day of the auction. His solicitor could carry out searches and other legal matters, although the terms and conditions of sale supplied with the specification will provide much of the same information his searches would otherwise reveal.

If a bid is accepted, the buyer must sign a document recording the sale, and pay a 10 per cent deposit, which is in effect the point where contracts are exchanged. This document – the Law Society's *Contract for Sale* – can also be included with the specification, together with a plan of the property. The period between the acceptance of the offer and the date for completion will be specified in the agreement.

As you can see, it is essential that you work closely with a suitably qualified person in order to undertake the role of selling agent where an auction is required.

Clinching the instruction

While you are actually at the property carrying out the valuation you should persuade the owner to instruct you to act for him. As soon as you leave, your chances of receiving the instruction are reduced. You immediately leave the door open for another agent.

Before you visit a property for the purposes of a market valuation, it is important to do your homework. That is, familiarise yourself with other properties for sale in the area and their prices for comparison, and also check your mailing list to see if you have any applicants looking for that type of property in that area. But never tell a seller you have a definite buyer unless this is perfectly true. You can often clinch an instruction, however, by pointing out that you have several people you are currently in touch with who are looking for this type of property. If they are in a position to go ahead quickly, this also increases your chances of an instruction.

Make it clear that you offer an efficient and first-class personal service, and point out all the other services you offer. Wherever possible, negotiate a sole agency instruction. Agency fees are based on the following instructions:

Sole agency
Here you are the only agent acting for the seller. A reduced fee is charged where a sole agency instruction is received, and it prevents the seller from instructing other agents at the same time. However, the seller may set a time limit on the instruction, after which he is at liberty to instruct other agents on the understanding that your fees will then revert to the norm. If the seller sells privately, no commission is due to you.

Sole selling rights
This means that you and you alone can sell the property, and your commission is due in the event of a sale, even if that sale was negotiated privately by the seller.

Multiple agency
These terms apply when the seller instructs more than one agent to act for him. Fees are set at their highest level for a multiple agency instruction and are payable to the agent who eventually sells the property.

Sub-agency
It is quite possible that you receive an instruction to sell a property which is perhaps out of your area, or for one reason or another is difficult to sell. In these circumstances you, as the main agent, may decide to sub-instruct another agent to assist you with the sale. You must confirm the agreement in writing to the other agent or agents you sub-instruct, together with confirmation of the terms of your commission arrangement with the seller, and enclose a copy of your specification from which the sub-agent can draw up his own.

If your sub-agent introduces a buyer to the property, the commission received on completion will be divided equally between yourself as main agent and the agent who made the introduction, unless an alternative arrangement has been made. If, however, he has nothing to do with the final sale, he receives nothing. Your sub-agent must make all viewing arrangements through you and it will be your responsibility to put forward an account for the final commission due. On receipt of your commission you must pay the sub-agent his portion of the fees if he made the introduction.

Although this agreement is between you and the other agent(s), it is a good idea to let the seller know about it and confirm it all in writing. No extra charge is made to the seller under these circumstances. If you are instructed to act as a sub-agent for someone else, you must confirm your acceptance of the arrangement in writing and draw up your own specification of the property from the main agent's copy. Follow his instructions with regard to viewing arrangements.

Your methods of advertising could well help towards obtaining the instruction. If a seller is familiar with your techniques, and they are successful, then there will be no problem, otherwise it is up to you to familiarise customers with your advertising methods. Use every option open to you – local and national advertising, local radio, magazines and editorials. You could even produce your own monthly review of the property available, and include a few helpful hints for home buyers and sellers, keeping them up to date with market trends.

More important, however, is your own approach to the client and his property. Show lack of interest, lack of knowledge and lack of attention and you are most unlikely to receive any instructions at all.

Confirming a valuation

It is important to confirm a valuation in writing. The letter should detail your services as well as confirm your assessment of market value. You should indicate that the price quoted relates to today's prices and may not apply at any other time. Give details of your commission structure and the terms and conditions under which your commission becomes payable, and don't forget to follow up the valuation in order to secure an instruction if it is not immediately forthcoming.

Preparing specifications

Measure up a property as soon as the instruction is received. If it is a multi-agency instruction, other agents may well move quickly and secure a sale before you have even taken details, so don't waste time.

Agents have their own methods of measuring up. Some prefer a tape to a rod-rule, while others invest in the more expensive lazer tape.

You may also prefer to dictate the details into a hand-held recorder, rather than write notes, but whichever method you choose, the outcome must still be the same: accurate and well-presented specifications.

Measurements can be taken in feet and inches or in metric measurements, or both, but if you measure right into bays or obscure corners, make sure you state maximum or minimum sizes.

The following details must be included:

- measurements of all rooms
- full details of the features of the room, for example, fireplace, fitted wardrobes or cupboards, display areas, window aspect
- details of light fittings and power points
- full description of type of central heating system
- colour scheme of sanitaryware
- detailed description of kitchen and fittings, and where built-in appliances are to be included, manufacturer's name should be indicated
- details of any guarantees which apply
- details of any outstanding planning consent
- measurements and details of garage and any outhouses
- measurement of plot and description of garden
- amount of rates payable, rateable value and water rates
- details of all services connected
- details of any septic tank on premises
- directions to get to the property
- proximity to shops, schools, public transport etc
- viewing arrangements – give your name here, but do not disclose if you hold a key for reasons of security
- full details of lease including number of years outstanding, ground rent, any other charges
- any other relevant comments or information.

It is also necessary to ascertain the needs and requirements of the seller – your client. He may, for instance, be purchasing another property and be anxious to find a buyer immediately, so eliminating the possibility of introducing a buyer still waiting to sell his own home. You need to find out the name and address of the seller's solicitor, together with the details of any chain in which he is involved. This will enable you to monitor progress carefully and make it a great deal easier to introduce a buyer who can fall in line with the special requirements of your client.

Another important point is that of access. It may be necessary to hold a key to gain access, and this is certainly worth suggesting to anyone who is at work all day or likely to be away for long periods, and is, of course, essential if the property is vacant. If the seller is still living in the property, make a note of any times when viewing would not be convenient, but point out to your client that 'spur of the moment' viewings often result in a sale. You also need a contact telephone number for the client both at home and business.

Next on your list is the difficult question of what is, or what is not, to be included in the asking price.

Items such as carpets and curtains are often included in the asking price. But it should be remembered that a building society will advance a loan on the value of the property, but not necessarily the fixtures and fittings left in it. The operative word here is *included* in the price. If the seller does intend to include them in the price, whether or not the purchaser actually wants them, then there is no reason why you should not mention this on your specification. On the other hand, the seller may wish to sell these items separately. Here you could mention that carpets, curtains or whatever other items are involved can be purchased by separate agreement, but on no account include on your specification anything which you are not one hundred per cent sure will remain. If you do, and the item is then removed, you could well be held responsible for its replacement.

Items such as carpets and curtains which are to be left in the property can well provide a good selling feature. They can also provide a point of negotiation which could be the difference between selling or not selling the property.

Presenting specifications

The first thing a purchaser will look for on a specification is a good colour photograph, the price, the number of rooms and any outstanding features of the property, and these should be clearly shown on the first page of the specification.

If these details seem of interest, the buyer will read on. Failure to provide an easy-to-read, eye-catching summary on the first page could result in the buyer not bothering to read any further.

You will undoubtedly be judged by the presentation of your specifications. If they are sent by post, and the recipients also receive the specification of the same property from another agent, they will no doubt choose to contact the agent whose presentation is the most professional.

A great deal will depend on the ability of your typist. If she is skilled and has a flair for presentation, then most of your worries are over. If not, it will be up to you to make sure that the format of your specifications is appealing, clear and easy to follow with no spelling errors or any other inaccuracies.

Don't, for instance, allow everything to be crammed on to one page. If two or more pages are necessary in order to ensure clarity, use them. Side headings indicating which room or part of the property is being described make it easy for the reader to find his way around. So, too, does a description starting from the front door and working through. It can get very confusing if the description begins on the top floor and wanders aimlessly about: the reader is unable to picture the relationship of one room to another. In any event, check the draft copy through carefully before you allow it to be copied and circulated.

An electric typewriter with a carbon ribbon will present a much clearer print than a manual machine. You will need to photocopy your specification and therefore the master copy must be as clear as possible. If finances stretch to it, a typewriter with a memory function will also be useful as some of your business letters will be to a standard format and can be coded into the machine. If you decide to invest in a word processing system, use a daisy-wheel printer in order to obtain the best possible reproductions.

Agents have different ideas about the display of prices on specifications when there has been a price reduction or alteration. Some will carefully change the original copy and re-run more copies for distribution, while others prefer to stamp 'Price Reduced' in large lettering over the original price. What we are looking for here is a well-presented copy, even if a rubber stamp is used. In the event of a price reduction, contact all those applicants who have shown interest and inform them of the change (which could be significant enough to encourage them to buy), and recirculate the amended specification. Readvertise, too, and don't forget to change the details in your window display.

A colour photograph of the external view of the property should be included on every specification, together with any other views which may be of special interest to your applicants. Photographs do not reproduce well if photocopied. However, you will need to circulate copies of the specification the day you receive the instruction and you will want to include a photograph on it. Because it is so important to distribute specifications immediately, it may be necessary to take a polaroid photograph which can be photocopied for the purposes of the mail-shot, as well as another photograph from which colour prints can be made. If you are unable to get the colour prints in time, a polaroid may well solve the immediate problem of getting the specification out the same day as the instruction.

Try to find someone locally who is able to provide a 'same day' service for you, and make sure you keep the negatives safely so that reordering can take place as necessary. Give someone the responsibility of checking particulars and making sure orders are placed for photographs *before* the previous batch has run out.

Under the Trade Descriptions Act 1968, a misrepresentation which is a false statement of fact made to persuade someone to enter into a contract is a criminal offence, and prosecution can result. It is therefore essential that somewhere on your specification – usually printed at the bottom – you include a statement to the effect that the particulars are produced in good faith although their accuracy is not guaranteed, nor does the specification constitute any part of a contract or warranty in relation to the property; applicants should personally inspect the property in order to satisfy themselves as to the correctness of the statements made. You may wish to consult your solicitor to establish the exact wording before your headed specification paper is printed.

Estate agents' jargon

We hear a lot about estate agents' jargon and it must be said that over the years estate agents have certainly invented a series of phrases all their own.

The important thing to remember while compiling your specification is that it must be accurate and truthful, but remember, too, that you are acting in the best interests of your client – the seller – and although you may think his home is a tip, you would not be inviting buyers if you said so in as many words. You could say instead 'in need of some decoration' or 'an ideal opportunity for the do-it-yourself enthusiast' or something similar, but don't say a property is in 'excellent decorative order' if it isn't, or 'suitable for a first-time buyer' if it is unmortgageable. Don't make a specification too flowery either. It makes the whole thing unreadable and silly. Just make sure you are as accurate as possible, and when you read through individual specifications with your applicants, that is the time to refer to any special points and explain that 'it does need decorating and tidying up, but that has been reflected in the price' – and of course, *take them to view.*

You must not misrepresent the property, so choose your words with care. Avoid jargon if you can and always be as accurate as possible.

Confirming the instruction in writing

A letter confirming the instruction is essential. The Estate Agents Act 1979 stipulates that an agent must tell his client what his charges will be and under what terms and conditions they will become payable. Failure to do so could result in the loss of your legal right to your charges, even if you successfully arrange a sale.

Your letter of confirmation should be sent immediately you receive the instruction. If it has not been received by the seller before you introduce a buyer, you could lose the right to claim your commission. Include full details of the terms of the agreement – sole agency, joint agency, sole selling rights (though this is not often used nowadays) – and any time constraints which may apply. This could be an arrangement where a sole agency has only been agreed for a limited period, after which your fees will revert to the norm. You may wish to reserve the right to sub-instruct another agent in which case make clear to the seller the terms under which commission would become payable. You could finish by assuring the seller that you will do your best to find a suitable purchaser, and inform him of the other services you are able to offer.

To avoid the problems which can result from sellers denying receipt of confirmation letters, many agents now include a second copy of the letter and ask the seller to sign it, indicating his approval and acceptance of the terms specified, and then return it to the agent as proof of acceptance. This is certainly a good idea, bearing in mind that if the seller denies having received the letter and you subsequently find a buyer who completes, he could refuse to pay your commission. Enclose a stamped addressed envelope with the letter too.

Changing market conditions

When mortgages are easily obtainable, and lenders are mounting elaborate advertising campaigns to encourage business, it usually brings about a period in the market when the demand for property exceeds supply. We then find ourselves with several prospective buyers for the same property, each making a higher offer in order to establish a purchase. This in itself pushes up prices generally, and brings about gazumping and contract races demanded by sellers so they get the highest possible price for their homes.

The other extreme is when mortgage finance is very limited and lenders find themselves unable to meet the demand. In this situation, long queues of borrowers form and agents are left with properties on their register which are not selling, through no fault of their own. Prices then level off and occasionally drop, bringing about a stagnant period. At times like these your in-house mortgage facilities can help. You may be in a position to push forward a mortgage application via the building society you represent, or a broker, and your applicant will be considered with some priority. It could even mean your customer avoids the long queue he would otherwise have found himself part of if he had applied for a loan direct.

When there are many properties available and few buyers, it becomes a 'buyer's market', for the buyer knows he can make a reduced offer for the property and the seller is more likely to accept it knowing the buyer can pick up a similar property elsewhere without much of a problem.

It is a 'seller's market' when there are only a few properties available to offer prospective buyers. Anxious buyers are then forced to make higher offers in order to secure any purchase at all.

Selling houses is traditionally a seasonal affair, and as we have already discussed, at certain times of the year property turnover is limited, while at others, the market changes again, and you will be rushed off your feet.

Leasehold properties

A freehold property means that the buyer will own the property and the land on which it stands. A leasehold property is somewhat different.

Leases usually run for a period of 99 or 999 years after which the ownership is passed back to the freeholder. The Leasehold Reform Act 1967 gives owners of leasehold houses the right to buy their freehold and this is an important point for the agent to remember.

Your approach to selling leasehold flats and maisonettes could, however, be slightly different. The first thing is to make sure you clearly distinguish the difference between a flat and a maisonette. A flat has a shared entrance or communal stairway of some kind, while a maisonette has its own. The problem is that some sellers prefer their property to be referred to as a maisonette rather than a flat!

The terms and conditions of leases are other important points to consider. Many sellers will not be able to give you much information about their leases, but it is wise to find out as much as you can in order to establish a realistic market value and to arm yourself with the sort of information a prospective buyer is likely to require.

Most important are the charges likely to be incurred by the buyer, and these include:

1. *The annual ground rent.* Often ground rent comes under review after a certain period, and it is usually increased at that time, so find out when the new review is due. If the term 'peppercorn' is used, it means nothing is payable.
2. *Maintenance charges.* These cover the upkeep of all shared facilities including the exterior of the building, driveways and forecourts, lifts, staircases and gardens.
3. *Insurance cover.* A share of the insurance cover for the whole building is usually payable. This cover, which is for fire and other risks, is arranged through the freeholder. It is also a wise precaution to find out where the owner's responsibility ends and the freeholder's begins in relation to damage.
4. *Other charges.* There could be a payment due for a shared central

heating or hot water system and also a charge for porterage or a security guard.

You must also find out the number of years left outstanding on the lease as this could affect the mortgageability of the property as does the floor level of the property.

The buyer's solicitor will check the terms of the lease very carefully, as each one varies, but nevertheless, it falls to you as the selling agent to provide as much information as you can.

You also need to find out about the following matters:

- which garage is allocated to the property and if there is a separate charge for the garage
- if there is no garage, is there allocated parking space and if so, where?
- where would visitors park?
- is there a communal garden, or a separate garden included with the property and, if so, are there any restrictions relating to the upkeep and/or use of the garden?
- what regulations apply to communal areas?
- does the landlord carry out his responsibilities to an acceptable standard (decorating and maintenance)?
- are there any other regulations which apply?

If you sell in an area where there are many leasehold properties, you may find it helpful to obtain from your local office of the Department of the Environment a free booklet called 'Service Charges in Flats' which explains the occupier's rights under the Housing Act 1980.

On-site sales

Many developers now have their own sales teams to market their properties. But many people buying newly built homes will have their own property to sell first. Some developers offer a part-exchange scheme for their customers in order to avoid a chain, and this is where a local selling agent is usually needed.

The developer will require a market valuation to be carried out by the agent, and he will base his part-exchange figure on a percentage of that valuation. He will then instruct the agent to sell the property in the normal way at the higher figure.

Fortunately, however, there are still many companies who engage agents to sell their homes, and here you could establish a sales area on site, or from a show home, as well as selling from your office. Be prepared to take on the responsibility of arranging choices of colour schemes, kitchen fittings and decor as offered by the builder, as well as carrying out all the other tasks associated with effective selling.

Your commission will have to be agreed and could be a set amount for each property sold, an overall amount for the whole site or a percentage commission for each property.

Selling new property does, of course, give you a good grounding on which to base advertising and encourages instructions from established properties, and in view of the fact that most people move house again within a five-year period, the efficient agent is most likely to receive those instructions too.

The only problem is that of staffing. Most site-sales offices are open all weekend and you may need to take on additional staff in order to provide coverage, especially if your own office is also open.

National House Building Council

All reputable builders and developers now belong to the NHBC, and their work must meet the standards laid down by the Council. Every property they build will be inspected and a numbered certificate/guarantee issued. Your buyer will not receive a mortgage advance unless the certificate is forthcoming.

The guarantee covers a period of ten years, during the first two years of which the builder is responsible for putting right any defects. However, if the builder should go bankrupt during that period, the Council will put right any defects arising from his failure to meet the standard of workmanship they require.

As a selling agent, it is worth remembering that builders often set dates for completion that they are eventually unable to meet. This can often cause a great deal of difficulty if chains of sales and purchases are affected, and often results in everyone having to change plans and alter arrangements at the very last minute. It is an unfortunate fact that there are still instances where buyers move into properties where painters and tilers are still at work. If you are representing the developer on site, you could well be the person to whom complaints are made, and although there is very little you can do, except perhaps redirect the complaint to the appropriate person, you must be prepared to deal with the situation in a fair and understanding manner.

Selling on behalf of executors

You may be instructed to sell a property on behalf of an executor, usually a solicitor. The executor is obliged to show that he obtained the best possible price for the property, but if someone has recently died in a house, it can sometimes make selling more difficult. Often, too, properties sold on behalf of executors are older and less desirable, and all this must be taken into account if you are asked to value the property for marketing purposes. The valuation must be confirmed in writing, and you must ensure that all offers are put forward, right up until contracts have been exchanged.

Property with part possession

Valuing a property with part possession is not always easy, and you may decide that in the interests of the seller the property should be put to auction.

Sitting tenants, on the other hand, may wish to purchase the property themselves, but usually this means they will offer a somewhat reduced amount. Investors are often interested in properties with part possession, basically in order to let the remainder of the building and secure an income from the transaction. However, a lot will depend on the terms written in to the existing tenancy agreement, which can also be influenced by the Rent Acts.

You need to establish, as far as possible, what these terms and conditions are, especially where the tenant is responsible for maintenance and repairs. A buyer will be anxious to know if the tenant must contribute towards these expenses. He will also want to know if the rent can be altered and whether the tenancy reverts to the landlord, or the heirs of the tenant, if the tenant should die.

The value of the property will depend, therefore, on the terms of the tenancy as well as the general size and condition of the property itself, and don't forget the mortgage conditions either. If the buyer requires a mortgage, he needs to check what percentage of advance the lender is likely to consider on a property with a sitting tenant, and make sure he is likely to get the amount he needs in relation to the purchase price.

Selling ex-council houses

The Housing Act 1980 and the Housing and Building Control Act 1984 give council tenants the legal right to buy their homes, and they are entitled to certain discounts based on the number of years they have occupied the premises. The details are outlined in a free leaflet called 'Your Right to Buy your Home – A Guide for Council, New Town and Housing Association Tenants', which can be obtained from the local authority or Citizens Advice Bureau.

Although this is unlikely to affect you as an estate agent, it is quite possible that the ex-council property will be put up for resale. An ex-council property in good condition can often provide good value for money from the point of view of the purchaser, but for the purposes of a market valuation and saleability, you must be aware of current selling prices for other ex-council houses, which are usually lower than similar properties in a private residential area.

Conclusion

An active and forward-thinking agent will soon build up a good register of properties and establish a steady flow of sales in relation to instructions received. He will encourage business by following up enquiries and valuations, and will establish himself firmly in the minds of buyers, so that when they sell in the future, they will return to him.

In today's competitive market-place, however, there is no room for error. You cannot afford to miscalculate when it comes to market valuations from a legal point of view and on the basis that you should be acting in the best interests of your client. Neither must you forget that swift action makes sales, many of which can be tied up to applicants already on your mailing list, even before the property is advertised.

Assignment 4: Securing instructions to sell

Objectives

- To identify weaknesses in your valuation techniques
- To put forward suggestions for improving techniques in order to turn every valuation into an instruction

Tasks

1. Produce a step-by-step report on four valuations you have carried out, explaining the criteria on which you based your valuation figure.
2. Give an account of what has happened since and whether you feel your original figure was correct. Explain your answer.
3. If you did not get an instruction from the valuation, analyse the reason or reasons for this.
4. List the steps you could have taken to secure the instruction.
5. Identify the common errors agents make when carrying out valuations, and say what legal position could result.
6. Put forward your own suggestions as to how your current methods of valuing property could be improved.

Assignment 5: Presentation of specifications

Objectives

- To ensure that your specifications are presented in a professional and acceptable manner at all times
- To identify areas where improvements can be made

Tasks

1. Take six specifications from your file and read them through carefully. Underline any typographical or spelling errors you find.
2. Check that the reproduction of the specifications is as clear as the original copy, and, if not, identify the reason for this.
3. Each copy should have a clear colour photograph. If it has not, find out why and suggest a method of ensuring that in the future *every* specification will have a photograph.
4. Suggest areas where the format and layout of your specification could be improved.
5. The exemption clause at the foot of your particulars must be clear and easy to read. How do you ensure that your customers understand what it means? What is the legal position regarding disclaimers?

Chapter 4

Your Role as Financial Adviser

Introduction

As a selling agent, it is your responsibility to find a buyer for your client's property who can see the transaction through to a satisfactory completion. To this end, you will be expected to help buyers not only to obtain mortgages, but also give them some idea what other costs they are likely to incur. Very few ordinary house buyers and sellers understand the complexity of mortgage packages and how they work, yet they will expect you, as the selling agent, to have a good working knowledge of mortgages and be in a position to answer all their questions about tax relief, surveys and conveyancing too.

It is quite surprising the number of people who agree to buy or sell property without any idea at all how much the transaction and all the associated fees are going to cost, and these are the people most likely to pull out of the deal when they finally find out. They may not actually *ask* you for advice along these lines, but nevertheless, in order to ensure that your sale moves forward, it is up to you to check as far as possible that the buyer's financial position is sound.

Unfortunately, over the last few years the number of people whose homes are being repossessed by lenders through non-receipt of mortgage repayments, or who are forced to sell because of increased running costs and expenditure, is steadily growing. Such cases are often affected by redundancy, or simply because lenders, anxious to strike a deal, make offers of advances which home buyers are quick to accept in order to complete their purchase, but at the same time they take little notice of the total monthly expenditure it ultimately leaves them with.

You may argue that your obligation is fulfilled as soon as you successfully complete a sale, and you would be right, of course. You might also say that each time a property comes up for sale, for whatever reason, it is good business for you. This is also true. But perhaps a little more carefully directed information regarding money matters during those early days would help the buyer to avoid a financial crisis later on.

The finances associated with buying a property stretch far beyond those to do with mortgages, and in this chapter we will be looking at these costs and how they are made up.

Arranging mortgages

It has been called the 'mortgage maze', which is probably an accurate description. The number and variations of advances currently available are quite staggering, and although the general principles are similar, the packages offered are structured in different ways.

If you are in a position to offer mortgages through the building society you represent, they will supply leaflets outlining the different schemes available, and you should study these carefully so that you feel confident in answering questions about them. If you introduce your applicant to a broker, he will have an in-depth knowledge of mortgage structures, and will also know where funds are currently available in order to place a suitable mortgage for the customer. However, this does not mean that you, as the agent, need not bother to find out which financial packages are likely to be suitable. Indeed, a certain mortgage package may well be necessary for a certain type of customer in order for him to complete the transaction, and you may need to take this into account before advising your seller to accept an offer from that customer.

As we discussed earlier, in order to negotiate a sale successfully, you must ascertain the purchasing capability of your buyers. Just because people say they want to buy a property doesn't necessarily mean that they can. As we know, one of the most common reasons for chains of sales and purchases falling through is because, somewhere along the line, someone has been unable to get the advance he needs. In order to avoid this unhappy situation, it is very important that the agent makes quite sure a mortgage is likely to be forthcoming before he completes negotiations and takes the property off the market.

The multiple system

If your prospective buyer has not yet made enquiries about the amount of money he can borrow, the first step is to work out a few figures for him to establish whether he is likely to get what he needs. You may have been provided with charts by the lender or broker you are in touch with, but if not, you must use the multiple system currently in operation.

All lenders use a multiple system of some kind in order to estimate how much they are willing to advance to their applicant. These multiples are directly linked to the applicant's annual salary and are also influenced by current interest rates. For instance, when interest rates are high the multiple is likely to be lower than when interest rates are low.

Multiples of a single gross salary can range from two to three times annual income, depending upon the current market situation. If your customers receive any additional income, perhaps by way of commission, overtime or bonuses, you could advise them to mention this to the lender when they apply for a loan, although this additional income must be received on a regular and continuous basis. If it is taken into consideration at all, it will probably only be in part.

Where a joint mortgage is applied for, the multiple system still applies, but again will vary from lender to lender. One lender may add both salaries together and multiply the total by two, while another lender may take the principal salary and multiply by two and half, and then add to this the secondary annual salary. These variations often give rise to one lender being prepared to offer slightly more money than another, which could mean the difference between your customer being able to purchase the property or not.

A single woman applying for a mortgage will be treated in exactly the same way as anyone else, and must have adequate income to support the advance, but a self-employed person must produce annual audited accounts, usually for a minimum period of the previous 12 months. Some lenders will demand accounts going back even further.

Most people want to buy the most expensive property they can afford, and it is therefore up to you, as the selling agent, to make sure they are not going to apply for an advance which they are obviously not likely to get. You would not be doing anything at all to help the seller if you agreed the sale, took the property off your books, and then found out the mortgage required was not realistic.

The 'in principle' mortgage offer

The selling agent's life is made a great deal easier when he receives an offer from someone who has already arranged a mortgage 'in principle', and has nothing to sell either.

Lenders, aware that many sellers are unwilling to accept offers from buyers who are not yet ready to make progress, are now prepared to confirm in writing the fact that they have agreed a mortgage in principle with their applicant.

This means, in fact, that they have interviewed the applicant, and are willing to make him an advance based on the information about salary and income so far received, but still subject to valuation and survey. They may also confirm when the money will be available, which is another important factor if the seller is anxious to negotiate a very quick completion in order to secure his own purchase. Where there is a contract race, or where there is the likelihood of gazumping, you will want to make sure *your* buyer completes in time, and if he has already arranged a mortgage in principle, and knows when the money is available, it will put him in a much stronger position to ensure completion and the security of your commission.

It is worth advising anyone making tentative enquiries about buying property to arrange a mortgage in principle as soon as they can.

The Homeloan Scheme

This scheme, backed by the government, has been designed to provide first-time buyers with additional finance in order to buy a property. It is a savings account which provides a tax-free bonus based on the amount of money saved. Savings must continue for a minimum of two years and there must be £300 in the account for at least one year before a mortgage is applied for. If the amount saved is £600 or over, an additional loan of £600 is made, and this can be added to the mortgage and is repayment and interest free for up to five years, after which the mortgage repayments are increased to account for the additional money. If the property is sold within the five-year period, the full £600 must be repaid (1987 figures).

There are many other savings schemes and 'clubs' currently being run by lenders specifically for first-time buyers. If you receive enquiries about finances from first-time buyers, you must encourage them to open a suitable account which could go a long way towards securing a mortgage at a later date.

Understanding mortgages

The following types of advances are the most popular packages currently available, although terms and conditions may vary slightly from lender to lender.

The repayment mortgage

This is also known as a capital repayment or annuity mortgage. Here the borrower's monthly repayments consist of part capital (the total amount borrowed) and part interest on the loan. At the beginning of the term, the repayments will consist almost entirely of interest, but as the term advances, more of the capital is paid off, and the proportion of capital to interest increases.

If interest rates rise during the term of the advance, the borrower is usually given the option to extend the term of the advance to cover the increase, without increasing the monthly repayments. However, this is not always a good idea, as it could mean that the term extends for an indefinite period. It is much better to increase the repayments to cover the increase in interest rates if this can be afforded. In the same way, if interest rates fall, the borrower can reduce his monthly repayments accordingly. If he continues to pay the higher rate, the term of the advance will decrease.

This type of advance must be accompanied by a mortgage protection policy which, in the event of a borrower's death, will pay off the outstanding amount of the loan.

Endowment mortgage

With an endowment mortgage, the capital is left outstanding throughout the term of the loan. None of it is paid off during that time. The advance is linked to an endowment policy and each month the borrower repays the interest on the loan, plus the premiums required for the policy.

The term of the policy must be equal to the term of the advance, and the insurance company from which the policy is obtained must be approved by the lender, so too must the policy itself.

At the end of the term, the endowment matures and is used to pay off the capital in full. There are several types of endowment policies which can be considered:

1. *A 'with-profits' endowment.* This type of policy provides enough money at the end of the term to pay off the capital sum in full. During the term of the advance it accrues bonuses based on the profits of the insurance company, and any money in excess of the amount needed to pay off the capital borrowed is paid to the borrower.

    Although quotations can be obtained for this type of advance, the figures quoted cannot be guaranteed. The eventual bonus payment will depend entirely on the profits of the insurance company.

2. *A 'non-profit' endowment.* This provides exactly the amount needed to pay off the loan at the end of the term. It also provides enough money to pay off the loan in full, should the borrower die before the term of the advance has expired. However, there are no additional bonuses at the end of the term.

3. *A low-cost endowment.* This type of mortgage is a little more risky for the borrower in as much as it is made up of a with-profits endowment policy which covers part of the amount of the advance only – usually about half. As bonuses are added to the policy, the amount covered increases, so that at the end of the term when the policy matures, there should be enough money to pay off the loan in full.

    This package is combined with a term insurance, so that should the borrower die before the loan is paid off, the insurance will cover the difference, ensuring that the full amount of the advance is paid off. Premiums for this type of package are lower than for the other types of endowment mentioned previously, but the borrower is gambling on the insurance company producing enough profits to provide adequate finances to pay off the loan at the end of the term.

If interest rates rise during the term of an endowment mortgage, repayments must be amended to ensure that the policy remains in line with the term of the advance.

If the borrower decides to move house before the end of the term, the policy can be transferred to the new property without the loss of bonuses so far accrued, and it can be extended to cover any additional advance the borrower requires. However, the first advance must be repaid in full from the profits of the sale, and another advance applied for in the usual way.

There are other options open to the borrower at this stage too. He can take out a repayment mortgage and still continue to pay the premiums on the endowment, so building up bonuses for the future, or he can turn his policy into a 'paid-up' policy. If he does this, he makes no further payments, but leaves his existing investment with the insurance company. The amount he has paid so far will continue to gain bonuses until the policy matures, but such bonuses will be considerably less than those expected if he continues to pay the premiums in full.

The borrower could also surrender the policy for a cash sum. However, this is unlikely to provide a good return if the policy is surrendered during the first few years.

Some lenders charge a slightly higher interest rate for an endowment mortgage than for a repayment mortgage.

Pension mortgage

A pension mortgage is available to people who are self-employed, or who do not participate in a company pension scheme. Instead of taking out an endowment policy, the borrower takes out a pension policy.

It is a system encouraging people to save towards retirement and which provides an income in retirement. Some of the funds can also be commuted into a cash sum which can be withdrawn free of tax on retirement.

The borrower will be entitled to tax relief on the payments made into the policy, unlike an endowment where there is no tax relief on the premiums paid. At the end of the term the policy matures to pay off the mortgage and provide a pension for life.

If the borrower's employment situation changes, and he becomes an employee participating in a pension scheme provided by the company, he is no longer entitled to the pension mortgage and must make other arrangements. He could, for instance, take out an endowment policy or transfer to an ordinary repayment mortgage. He should consult his insurers and decide which option would be most beneficial.

Low-start mortgage
This type of advance is usually restricted to first-time buyers. At the beginning of the term, the repayments are lower, and gradually increase as the term advances.

Some insurance companies combine a low-start scheme with a low-cost endowment. In some cases, the repayments increase over the term of the policy, but the maximum repayment is usually reached after five or ten years. Terms and conditions vary, but basically the system is designed for first-time buyers whose status and employment prospects are likely to improve, thus enabling them to increase their repayments as time progresses. However, if a husband and wife take out a low-start mortgage when they are both working, and the wife then leaves full-time employment, perhaps to start a family, the increase in repayments could become due at that time and the borrower could possibly find them difficult to meet.

Guaranteed mortgage
This is a system encouraging people to save with a lender on a regular basis. It guarantees a mortgage advance based on savings, and the mortgage figure is calculated by multiplying the total saved by an amount set by the lender. This could be as much as ten times the savings.

As for any investment, the investor will receive interest on his money, but he must save regularly for a set period of time before applying for an advance. The lender will then make the advance, subject to survey in the usual way. The investor can also withdraw his savings if he needs to.

Top-up advances
A top-up advance is in effect a second mortgage, and the lender will have second call on the property for the purpose of security for the advance.

If your customer is unable to raise the required amount of capital through the main lender, he could possibly arrange a top-up advance from another source, usually via an insurance company or perhaps a bank. However, some lenders will make it a condition of the first advance that a second advance from another source is not acceptable.

Interest rates are higher for a top-up, and a solicitor will have to be paid extra fees for handling the legal work. Your customer may also have to pay the solicitor acting on behalf of the second lender. Additional insurance will be required to cover the extra loan, and all this adds up to an expensive way of borrowing money.

Local authorities as lenders
Some local authorities are prepared to offer mortgages, but only very

rarely, as their funds are usually limited, and people buying their own council property will receive priority. However, if the property itself is not up to a good mortgageable standard, a local authority may be prepared to consider an application for an advance. If they are unable to meet demands, the authority may refer the applicant to a lender who operates the Building Societies' Association Support Scheme. The referral must come through the local authority and will depend upon income and the circumstances which prevail. If you approach your local authority, they will let you know how they operate and what rules and regulations they apply.

Private loans
Your customer may be arranging a private loan, perhaps through his family, or perhaps through a solicitor, broker or even an accountant. The terms and conditions of a private loan must be agreed and documented, and could include a calling-in clause which will specify the length of notice the lender has to give the borrower when he requires his money back in full. This type of agreement is made through a solicitor, and in order to check out the position of your buyer, you will have to contact the solicitor direct.

Loans from employers
Some employers are able to subsidise employees' monthly repayments by an agreed amount, or offer their employees special rates of interest on advances. Building societies and banks, for instance, are able to do this for their employees. However, if the borrower leaves that employment, his repayments will have to return to the normal rate or he may find it necessary to take out a loan from another source. Here, again, if your buyer says he is arranging his finance through his company, check it out with his solicitor.

Banks as lenders
Mortgage arrangements can be made through the borrower's bank, and some banks now oversee chains of estate agents and provide advances for their customers' needs.

If your customer applies direct to his bank, a multiple system will be used to calculate the amount he can borrow. Some banks charge an 'arrangement fee' for the mortgage. This could be a set charge or a fee based on the amount of the advance. Interest rates are variable and there is a range of mortgage packages available to the applicant. Some banks will confirm to selling agents whether a mortgage is likely to be obtained, but if not, check with your customer's solicitor.

Tax relief

Tax relief is available on the interest paid on advances up to £30,000 (1988 figure). Advances above that amount do not qualify for relief.

A married couple are restricted to relief up to £30,000, but single people can claim relief up to £30,000 each on loans taken out before 1 August 1988. After that date, only one claim for tax relief per property can be made, even where a property is purchased jointly.

The MIRAS scheme – mortgage interest relief at source – was introduced by the government in April 1983. Under this scheme, the borrower's monthly repayments are reduced by the amount of tax relief to which he is entitled, and the lender claims the difference from the Inland Revenue. Therefore, reductions in the rate of tax need to be offset by an increase in monthly repayments.

Borrowers who pay tax at the higher rate will get basic relief through MIRAS, and relief at the higher rate through their tax coding.

Most lenders calculate the net repayment on advances to remain constant throughout the term of the advance, even though throughout the term the level of interest paid on the outstanding amount varies. Some banks will expect the full amount to be paid, and will reimburse the borrower's current account with the tax relief which is due. This method allows for maximum tax relief when the maximum amount of interest is being paid during the early part of the loan, but it gradually decreases in ratio.

Tax relief on premiums for life insurance policies including endowments was abolished in March 1984, although any policy taken out before that time still qualifies.

If you are lucky enough to have a computer system which calculates mortgage repayments both net and gross, and supplies your customer with a print-out of expected bonuses and so on, life will be a great deal easier. If not, then you will have to rely on repayment charts to give your customers an accurate assessment of what they can expect their monthly repayments to be in relation to the amount of the advance, and the term over which the advance is to run. Lenders and brokers will provide written quotations on request.

Even though you may refer your applicant to a broker to effect the application, you should still be in a position to calculate these figures yourself, especially if the broker is not always immediately available to deal with the enquiry for you. Having such information readily available could mean the difference between closing the sale and losing your customer to another agent.

Interest rates

It is important to make clear to your customer that any figures you quote are based on current interest rates, and on the term of the advance. Wherever possible, the figures you quote should show the monthly repayment due when tax relief has been deducted at source as well as the gross amount, but you must stress that interest rates will fluctuate during the term of the advance and this will affect the figures at that time. Remind the borrower that although the term over which a repayment mortgage is paid off can be extended to meet any increase, this is not so in the case of an endowment, where the policy must remain in line with the advance and an increase must be met.

Some lenders also bring in threshold figures, above which a higher rate of interest is charged. For instance, one lender may charge an extra 0.5 per cent on a loan above £20,000 and a further 0.5 per cent above £25,000. Another may only impose a higher rate when the figure of £30,000 is reached.

The term of the advance

The number of years over which the loan can run will depend upon the age of the applicant. There is a choice, but most lenders will expect the loan to be paid off by the time the borrower retires. The usual maximum term is 25 years, although some lenders will extend this, but it is assumed that most people move house several times during their lifetime, and at each move, one loan must be paid off before another can be taken out.

For a young couple or first-time buyer, the maximum term available can be obtained, but for older people, it is sensible to reduce the term in order to ensure the loan is paid off on retirement.

Understanding the constraints

In order to produce a completed sale, it is important for the agent to relate the nature of his buyer's mortgage to the property itself. Failure to do so could result in the negotiations breaking down at a later date and the sale being lost.

There are many reasons why a sale could fall through due to problems arising from the mortgage application.

If the customer needs to borrow a high percentage of the total purchase price, you must make sure the property will stand up to survey. We have already discussed in Chapter 3, the restrictions lenders apply to loans, and if the property to be mortgaged could fall into one of the categories mentioned, then a high advance in relation to the asking price is not likely to be forthcoming; unless more money can be raised towards the purchase by the buyer, it would not be advisable to arrange a sale to him.

From experience you will soon learn which lenders look favourably on which type of property and in which area. If your customer has problems with a retention or a down-valuation, you could save the day by placing the mortgage elsewhere.

As you can see, your knowledge and understanding of the way mortgages work are essential if you are to negotiate sales which finally complete.

Mortgage guarantee policy

As we know, the lender will instruct a surveyor to carry out a valuation of the property to be mortgaged in order to make sure the property is sound security for the advance required. It will be upon this valuation figure that an offer of an advance will be made.

If the loan required is in excess of the normal maximum advance made by the lender – usually 75 to 80 per cent of the valuation figure – additional security will be required by the lender to cover the difference.

Where 100 per cent advances are advertised by lenders the amount of the loan above the set percentage of valuation is covered in this way.

This security takes the form of a mortgage guarantee policy, or indemnity policy, which the lender arranges through an insurance company. The insurers guarantee the lender against any loss he might incur by advancing the extra amount.

The borrower will have to pay for the premium and this is usually added to the loan and repaid over the term of the mortgage. The figures will be outlined in the mortgage offer when it is received.

Insurances

There are certain insurances which your customers must take out to protect both themselves and their families and to cover the property itself. Although your customers will no doubt have cover suited to their particular circumstances, the following insurances must be included:

Mortgage protection insurance

A repayment mortgage must be accompanied by a mortgage protection insurance. The policy provides enough money to pay off the mortgage in full if the borrower dies before the end of the term of the advance.

A *decreasing term policy* allows for the sum insured to be decreased as the term of the advance continues, leaving just enough money to pay off the outstanding amount of the loan at any one time. It is important for the borrower to make sure that the cover is still sufficient if interest rates are changed.

A *convertible term policy*, however, enables borrowers to change from a term policy to another type, such as an endowment, if they wish to do so.

The *level term policy* provides a fixed amount of cover for the full period of the advance.

Usually a lender will expect the policy to be assigned to him. If he does not, in the event of the death of the policy-holder, the money will go directly to the heirs, who then have the choice of paying off the mortgage or continuing to pay the monthly repayments as before, leaving them with a lump sum.

Most lenders will arrange the necessary mortgage protection policy for the borrower, but any insurance company providing the cover must be approved by the lender.

Building insurance

It is a condition of any mortgage that adequate insurance in the form of a house building policy is taken out.

In the event of a disaster such as a fire or flood, the policy should cover the cost of rebuilding the property. The lender usually arranges the cover, and the borrower becomes responsible for the cover from the day on which contracts are exchanged. The lender pays the first premium from that date, and the amount is added to the mortgage and the figures adjusted accordingly. This, too, will be shown on the mortgage offer.

As the price of materials and rebuilding costs increase, so too must the building insurance. Premiums are due once a year and at that time they should be increased in line with rising costs. Most policies are index linked anyway, and the lender will notify the borrower of the amount required. Lenders base their estimates on the House Rebuilding Cost Index, which is provided by the Royal Institution of Chartered Surveyors and is recalculated every year.

You should explain to your customer the importance of this cover, and suggest that he should check each year that the amount of cover provided is adequate. He should also read the small print carefully to make sure he understands fully what the policy covers and how any claims should be made.

Endowment policies

In addition to allowing the mortgage to be repaid in full in the event of the death of the borrower, an endowment policy also provides enough money to pay off the outstanding amount of the loan at the end of the term of the advance.

The policy will have to be assigned to the lender, and when it matures he takes from it the amount he needs to repay the loan and any money left over is paid to the borrower.

There are other types of endowment policies which do not relate directly to mortgages, and your customers can obtain details from their insurance company or from your broker.

Depending on the terms of your arrangement with the broker, or even directly with an insurance company, you could earn commission if you introduce someone who takes out insurance with or without mortgage.

Household policy

The British Insurance Association supply a leaflet called 'A Guide to Home Contents Insurance'. This sets out all the items which a householder is likely to own and which should be insured against risks, such as theft, fire, flood, riots, explosions and subsidence.

Although it is not a condition of mortgage to have such cover, it is obviously in the interests of your customers to take out a suitable policy with the insurance company of their choice.

It is surprising how the value of house contents and personal possessions mount up, and adequate cover is essential. The policy should be dated from the day your customer takes possession of his new property, and special valuables such as jewellery, paintings and so on should be assessed for insurance purposes on a regular basis to ensure that the amount of cover increases with inflation.

The right advice for your customer

A particular type of mortgage package could well suit one person, but not another, and much will depend on the status and age of the applicant.

All you can do as an agent is to offer guide-lines to the choices available and how they work in principle. The final decision must be left to the customer and take into account any changes in his life-style which may affect his income during the period of the advance.

You should be able to give some indication of the amount of money he is likely to be able to borrow, based on the multiple system currently being operated by the lenders you are in touch with, and the number of years the advance is required for. Until your customer has this figure, it is difficult for him to assess what price property to look for. As we said, most people buy the most expensive home they can afford, so the chances are they will look at property above their expected purchasing ability and then make an offer. What you need to do as the agent is to make sure that if the offer is accepted, the chances of obtaining the necessary advance are good. Failure to do so could result in the sale falling through, and this is something you need to avoid at all costs, especially if you have a chain of sales linked to the negotiation.

Very few buyers fully understand the constraints which apply to loans, and it is fair to say that sellers are usually in the same position. It is therefore up to you to point out to all concerned anything to do with the property that could cause a problem in relation to the buyer obtaining an advance.

What other expenses will your customer face?

You will often be asked how much all the fees and expenses are likely to cost, and in order to provide some sort of guide-lines, you must understand how each fee is made up and why it has to be paid.

The initial expense for the buyer is:

Valuation and inspection fees

As soon as the buyer completes his mortgage application form, he will be asked to pay an inspection/valuation fee which must be submitted with the form. Cheques must be made payable to the lender and not to the lender's agent, whether this is you, a broker or anyone else.

Fees for this are graded in relation to the purchase price of the property to be inspected, and the type of survey the buyer chooses.

The basic inspection/valuation is arranged by the lender and is carried out for the benefit of the lender in the first instance. He instructs a surveyor to inspect the property to make sure it provides sound security for the amount of the advance applied for, and that the property is a good investment for the lender.

The amount of the actual advance will be based on the valuation figure, and will be 75 or 80 per cent of that figure. As we have already mentioned, an advance above that percentage will require additional security to cover the balance.

A copy of this basic report is usually sent to the borrower, but it must be remembered that this is a very *basic* report and is not likely to contain as much information as a more detailed survey. If the borrower requires a more extensive survey to be carried out, this can be arranged through the lender at the same time, although an additional amount to cover the cost will have to be paid.

Neither the building society nor the surveyor will give any warranty or assurance that the conclusions or statements made in the report are accurate or reliable, so your customer may also request a private survey to set his mind at rest.

Newly built property

If the property to be mortgaged is still in the course of construction, the lender may release the advance in a series of stages.

Application is made in the usual way, and detailed plans of the property are also submitted for inspection. The money is released as building work continues. At each stage of the work the lender will inspect the property to ensure it is up to the required standard, and a certain amount of the advance will be made. The borrower must pay interest on the loan from the time it is first received, and most lenders charge a separate inspection fee for each stage.

House Buyer's Report and Valuation

This is a more detailed survey, and it is suitable for modern houses and bungalows up to 2,000 square feet in floor area, and no more than three storeys high.

The Royal Institution of Chartered Surveyors House Buyer's Report and Valuation must be carried out by a professionally qualified surveyor, and the inspection covers all the parts of the property to which the surveyor can gain easy access, or that he can easily see and reach.

Although the report is unlikely to list every minor problem, it will certainly bring to light any serious defects, and the surveyor will recommend further investigations or suggest courses of action which should be taken.

You could put your customer in touch with a surveyor who carries out this type of survey, or your customer can arrange it through the lender when he applies for a mortgage. If he does this, the surveyor will carry out both the valuation and the report at the same time, but the applicant will have to pay the additional fee for the report.

Such a report provides the buyer with an accurate assessment of the current market value of the property, as well as indicating any problems which require further investigation.

Flat Buyer's Report and Valuation

The Royal Institution of Chartered Surveyors Flat Buyer's Report and Valuation is similar to the above, but has been specially devised for people buying leasehold flats and maisonettes.

The property can be purpose built or a converted flat or maisonette, and the surveyor will report on all parts of the property to which he can gain access. However, you should point out to the buyer that the surveyor may not be able to gain access to certain parts of the building which are not part and parcel of the flat itself, and therefore his survey will not cover these areas.

If you, or the buyer, have been able to obtain a copy of the lease, it is useful to let the surveyor have a look at it, so that he can take into account the terms, conditions and charges connected with the lease when he makes his market valuation.

It should be remembered that both these reports will be limited to the areas to which the surveyor can gain access or can see. He will not lift fitted carpets or move furniture. He will, where possible, visually inspect electrical wiring and remove drain covers for inspection, but an in-depth report on the condition of these must be provided by a professional plumber or electrician. However, the surveyor will certainly advise further inspection by a suitably qualified person if he thinks it is necessary.

The surveyor will also give his opinion as to whether the agreed purchase price is realistic, bearing in mind his report, and major defects will be noted and listed in general terms.

Fees for both the above types of inspection are scaled in relation to the purchase price of the property, and written confirmation of the conditions under which the surveyor is engaged should be obtained by the applicant and are set out on the application forms.

A full structural survey

This is a much more thorough inspection of the property and will show every defect. It covers all parts of the property to which reasonable access can be obtained and will provide a detailed report on the general condition of the property and any defects that come to light.

Bearing in mind that there are very few properties – even new ones – which are absolutely perfect, you should warn the applicant that faults will undoubtedly be found. This is, after all, what the surveyor is looking for. He will list all these faults and recommend testing of installations such as electrical wiring or drainage if he thinks this is necessary. He will also suggest that specialists are called in if he detects a potential problem which he feels requires expertise in a certain field, such as timber treatment.

The survey will include the following points:

- the construction of the property
- state of the roof, including tiles, slates, insulation, chimneys and flues
- condition of woodwork throughout the property, including any evidence of wet or dry rot, woodworm
- condition of plumbing, including fittings in bathroom, toilet, kitchen waste pipes, water tanks

- rainwater goods, including gutters and downpipes
- electrical installation and wiring throughout the property
- soundness of foundations, including any sign of settlement or subsidence
- drainage system
- report of evidence of damp – rising damp, damp-proof course, other related problems
- condition of walls both external and internal, plasterwork, brickwork, pointing, cracks
- general description of decorative state
- garden and outbuildings, including paths, walls and fences and, where appropriate, inspection of swimming pool
- recommendations for specialist inspection as appropriate
- recommendations for testing of any likely problematic areas, such as wiring or central heating system.

The applicant will have to pay an additional fee for any specialist inspection recommended by the surveyor.

If your customer is thinking of knocking walls down, or extending the property, or altering it in any way, he should discuss these plans with the surveyor before the survey is carried out. The surveyor will, for instance, check which are load-bearing walls and make sure the property can stand up to any alterations the applicant has in mind.

The surveyor will also report on the general location of the property, and any factors which may affect the property itself and/or its value.

Because a surveyor can be liable for a claim for negligence if he overlooks a defect which is later discovered, he is always very careful to ensure that every little detail is included in his report. The final report your customer will receive will therefore include many minor defects as well as the more serious, or potentially more serious, problems, and will be extremely comprehensive.

Many people who instruct surveyors are horrified when they receive their report, generally because of the number of minor defects which come to light. The first person they run to is often the selling agent, either having decided to withdraw from the deal altogether in view of the report or demanding that the seller reduces the price in order to cover the costs of having the work carried out.

You don't want to lose your sale, but do bear in mind that you want the best for the seller, and although you may be able to save the sale by renegotiating a lower purchase price, you might also do better for the seller if you were to find another buyer who does not want a full structural survey and is prepared to accept the property as it stands, subject only to valuation. This does not mean that the problems go away, only that you find a purchaser less likely to be panic-stricken if he receives a surveyor's report showing many of the minor problems that nearly all homes have.

The fees for a full structural survey are usually negotiable and are based on the age of the property as well as the price.

Receiving inspection fees and checking mortgage application forms

If you supply the mortgage application form, the chances are that the applicant will return it to you to send on to the lender, or if he has a query regarding his application, he may well come to you for help, rather than go straight to the lender.

It is important to stress that every part of the mortgage application form must be completed in full. Failure to do so could result in the form being returned to the applicant, and precious time being wasted before things get under way again.

Mortgage application forms are generally divided into two main parts – the first appertaining to the applicant and his personal details, the second to the property itself. Where an application is put forward in joint names, all names and personal details of each applicant must be included on the form. The form will include questions relating to:

- name, address, telephone number both at home and work of each applicant
- marital status of each applicant
- purpose of the mortgage
- anticipated date of retirement
- amount required
- amount of applicant's own money to be contributed
- term required
- type of mortgage (repayment or endowment)
- first-time buyer
- if first-time buyer, will applicant apply for benefits in relation to the government's Homeloan Scheme?
- date of birth
- number and details of dependants likely to reside in the property
- occupation and details of promotion prospects
- length of service in present occupation
- name and address of employer with name of contact person or staff number
- total annual income
- details of any additional income, how it is received and for what

- details of any heavy financial commitments such as hire purchase
- full address of property to be purchased
- description of property, ie house, bungalow, flat
- age of property
- if leasehold, full details of lease including expiry date
- construction of property, ie brick and tile, cob and thatch
- names of anyone likely to reside in the property apart from the applicants themselves
- their relationship to the applicant
- name and address of seller
- name and address of selling agent
- details of how access can be obtained to the property for the purposes of a survey (the agent's name must be given here if a key is being held for access)
- name and address of buyer's solicitor
- details of any additional survey the applicant requires
- details of sale of existing property and how it has progressed so far
- if the applicant is self-employed:
  - audited accounts will be required for at least the previous 12 months, if not longer
  - name of business
  - address of business
  - nature of business
  - date business established
  - name and address of accountant and/or bankers
- if the property is in the course of construction:
  - name and address of builder, or
  - name of supervising architect.

The inspection fee *must* be submitted with the form, and a scale of fees is usually provided by the lender. The cheque your customer makes out must be made payable to the lender and not to you or a mortgage broker. If your applicant requires additional surveys to be carried out at the same time, you should check with the lender how much this is going to cost in order to include the additional amount with the application. If he has not already done so, the lender will request an interview with the applicant.

On receipt of the completed application form and inspection fee, the lender will require written confirmation of the applicant's income. In most cases the lender writes to the employer requesting the confirmation and when this is received, the surveyor is instructed to carry out the valuation. The theory is that if these initial enquiries are not satisfactory, the survey fee will not be used and will be returned to the applicant. However, most negotiations need to be concluded as quickly as possible and therefore the applicant may need to stress to the lender that in order to expedite the proceedings, the surveyor should be instructed as soon as possible.

It is worth mentioning to the applicant that he should leave instructions with his company to pass on the information requested by the lender as soon as possible. All too often, a busy personnel officer will leave an enquiry letter lying around for a few days before he gets round to doing anything about it, causing further delays and frustration. If your applicant gives permission for his personal details to be released, rather than the personnel department seeking him out to get such permission, even more time can be saved. You may even suggest that the applicant lets you know when the application has been received by his company as this will help you monitor progress.

Once a survey has been carried out, and other matters relating to the application have been finalised, the lender will issue an offer of an advance – a mortgage offer – setting out the amount of the loan, how that amount is made up, the term of the advance and any other relevant details. Figures shown will take into account, as appropriate, insurance, guarantee bonds, retentions or down-valuations, and will set out the terms and conditions under which the offer is made.

In view of all the other elements taken into account when the written offer is made to the applicant, the figures may not be in line with those the applicant expected, and he may well turn to you for an explanation rather than to his solicitor or the lender. It is certainly worth directing the applicant towards his lender or solicitor for advice, but here again, precious time could be wasted and you may consider it more appropriate to run through the offer with the applicant yourself, explaining the figures – which are easy to decipher by those who understand them – and setting the applicant's mind at rest. If he is still not satisfied, then his solicitor should be contacted for advice.

As soon as the offer is accepted by the applicant – and fully understood – he should sign the form as indicated, and return it to the lender as soon as possible.

If you are not involved in this yourself, ask the buyer to let you know as soon as the offer has been returned to the lender so that you can inform the vendor and keep track of the negotiations. If there seems to be a delay then you need to find out why and take appropriate action.

Where down-valuations or retentions come to light, your buyer may consider pulling out of the deal, in which case you may have to renegotiate a more acceptable purchase price with the vendor in order to save the sale. If this happens, don't forget to confirm any change of agreed purchase price to the seller and his solicitor, the buyer and his solicitor and, if appropriate, to the buyer's lender.

Legal expenses

As a selling agent you should be aware of the expenses your customers are likely to incur with regard to the legal side of the negotiations, and what those charges are for. You may also be asked to recommend a solicitor or a conveyancer to undertake your customer's case. This can sometimes leave you in a rather difficult situation in that although you would like to recommend a legal adviser, from your point of view it is much safer to direct your customer along several lines, so that he makes the final choice, just in case anything goes wrong. As you follow up sales and keep in contact with local solicitors and conveyancers, you will soon learn who are the most effective and who move the quickest. However, it is sad to say that not all legal advisers work as quickly as their customers would like; not that it is always their fault, but often due to heavy workloads, or simply because they are never in their offices when they are most wanted.

Solicitors have long held the monopoly for conveyancing, but in recent years the number of companies who specialise in conveyancing and do nothing else has steadily grown, bringing about a change of attitude towards the matter both from legal bodies and from consumers. It must be said that the competition with regard to charges for conveyancing has certainly done no harm, and since 1984, when the Law Society first allowed solicitors to advertise their services too, that competition has continued to be strongly felt.

Conveyancers are members of professional organisations and must have indemnity insurance to protect their clients' accounts, must undergo training, and most set a standard fee for the work, based on the price of the property. Only qualified licensed conveyancers or solicitors are entitled to draft conveyancing documents and charge a fee. Since December 1987, licensed conveyancers have also been able to draft contracts. It is unlawful for an unqualified person to do so for a fee. Solicitors no longer use the scale fees laid down by the Law Society for Conveyancing. However, their charges must be fair and reasonable and if your customers ask for a quotation, they should check whether the price quoted is a fixed sum or just an estimate.

Both solicitors and conveyancing companies will provide quotations for carrying out the legal work for your customers, and there is certainly no harm in shopping around for the best deal, bearing in mind that such an important matter must be approached with care and competence.

As well as a fee for carrying out the work, other standard charges will apply. These include:

Stamp duty
This is paid by the buyer and is a tax on legal documents. It is currently 1 per cent of the purchase price, if that price is over £30,000 (1988 figure). If the property is being purchased for less, no stamp duty is required.

In cases where a property is selling for around that figure, but the purchase of extras, such as fitted carpets and curtains, pushes the price up above £30,000, you could suggest that the buyer pays a separate amount for the extras, leaving the price of the property itself below the amount upon which the duty becomes payable.

Land Registry fees
Another fee paid by the buyer. Not all properties are as yet registered with the *Land Registry Office*. If the property to be purchased is registered, the fee will be slightly less than for first registration.

The Land Registry contains all the details of the property and its land, the names of previous owners, in fact everything a solicitor will need to know to establish the true ownership of the property and verify that the seller is legally entitled to sell it. The accuracy of the register is guaranteed by the state, and therefore if a property is registered, it makes the solicitor's life much easier. If the property is unregistered, the buyer's solicitor will have to investigate the title deeds for the last 15 years in order to establish a 'good root'.

If the property has not been registered, the buyer's solicitor will register the title on completion of the deal.

The compulsory registration of land was established by the repealed Land Transfer Acts of 1875 and 1898 and extended by the Land Registration Acts 1925–71. Most areas have now established compulsory registration, but there are still some properties which remain unregistered, and when these are sold the fee for first registration will apply.

Mortgage redemption charge
This may have to be paid by the seller if he redeems (pays off) his mortgage and does not take out another advance from the same lender. Some lenders, but not all, make this charge which can be an additional three months' interest on an advance when it is paid up within the first few years of the advance.

Mortgagee's legal expenses
Paid by the borrower. This fee is charged by the lender for the legal work involved in drawing up the mortgage deeds, but if the borrower's own solicitor also acts for the lender, the fee could be slightly lower.

Local authority search fees

Paid by the buyer for searches made by the solicitor in connection with any planned development in the area of the property to be purchased, rights of way across the land, if the property has valid planning permission, or any other factor which may affect the property and its land. Because local authorities do not usually act with any great speed, it can take some time for solicitors to receive replies to searches – yet another point of delay to be taken into account.

Arrangement fee

Paid by the borrower. Building societies do not usually charge a fee for arranging a mortgage, but some banks do. The amount is based either on the purchase price of the property, or the amount of the loan, or a set standard fee.

Removal costs

Your customers may decide to move themselves, or to engage the services of a removal company.

A removal company that is a member of the British Association of Removers is generally a good choice, and suitable insurance cover can be arranged under the Association's block policy. Charges are based on the amount to be moved and the length of the journey.

Charges for hiring a van are based on a fixed sum per day with unlimited mileage, or a smaller fixed sum with an additional charge per mile. A deposit will have to be left and the hire company will want to see the applicant's driving licence. A vehicle up to 7.5 tonnes laden weight can be driven on an ordinary driving licence.

Your selling fees

Paid by the seller. You will need to know when exchange of contracts takes place. Usually solicitors notify the selling agent and ask for an invoice to be forwarded to them for the appropriate fees their client has to pay. If you don't receive such a letter, it is important to find out exactly when contracts have been exchanged and make up an invoice. You must add VAT to your charges, and the invoice is sent to the seller's solicitor and is taken into account when he submits his *final account* to the client.

When he has completed all the formalities, and the money has been received in respect of the sale, the seller's solicitor will issue you a cheque for your commission.

Occasionally, an agent makes a special arrangement with the seller at the beginning of the negotiations, whereby the seller pays the agent direct. Your invoice must be sent direct to the seller, so make sure you have a forwarding address and confirm the arrangement in writing with your letter of confirmation for the instruction, so that it is signed by the seller thus acknowledging his acceptance of the agreement right from the word go. However, sending a bill direct to the seller often causes delays in receipt of commission, and it is much safer to put forward an account via the seller's solicitor in the usual way.

DIY conveyancing

There is absolutely no reason why your customer should not undertake his own legal work, but unless you know that he has some practical experience, or is capable of carrying out the work to a good standard, it may not be a good idea to encourage him. It will certainly save him some money, but in view of the implications of an error or an oversight of some kind, do-it-yourself conveyancing should not be undertaken by a beginner, although he could always fall back on the experience of the professionals if he really comes unstuck. The problem from your point of view could be that the seller is reluctant to agree a sale in view of any pending difficulties or hold-ups associated with the buyer fumbling through and causing delays.

Bridging finance

At the time contracts are exchanged your buyer will have to pay 10 per cent of the purchase price as a deposit. If he cannot pay this from his own resources, his bank will probably lend him the money for the short period between exchange and completion and provided a contract is forthcoming.

Interest will be charged on the loan, which must be repaid on completion. The buyer should consult his bank manager and his solicitor to finalise the details and establish the rate of interest which will apply.

Budget plans for your customers

Helping your customers to budget properly will depend upon their individual circumstances. Many people will prefer to work it all out on their own – finances are, after all, a very personal thing – and they may not wish to discuss it with you. Nevertheless it is part of your responsibility towards your seller to make sure, as far as you can, that a sale is only negotiated to someone who is not likely to back out at the last minute due to lack of funds. To this end the wise agent will put together a formula outlining the basic expenditure likely to be incurred by buyers and sellers alike.

Here are some suggestions you may find helpful:

Budget plan for buyers only

Expenses

Valuation/inspection fee, including VAT	£
Other survey fees if required, including VAT	£
Mortgage arrangement fee if required	£
Legal fees, including VAT	£
Indemnity/guarantee bond as required	£
Removal costs including VAT	£
Small contingency fund for unexpected extras	£
TOTAL EXPENSES	£
Amount of personal money to be included	£
Amount of mortgage which can be raised	£
TOTAL AMOUNT AVAILABLE	£

Budget plan for customers who are buying and selling at the same time

Expenses

Amount due to repay existing mortgage	£
Mortgage redemption charge if applicable	£
Mortgage arrangement fee if required	£
Legal fees, including VAT	£
Indemnity/guarantee bond as required	£
Removal costs, including VAT	£
Estate agent's commission, including VAT	£
Small contingency fund for unexpected extras	£
TOTAL EXPENSES	£

Anticipated selling price of property	£
Amount of personal money to be included	£
Total amount available	£
LESS expenses	£
Total amount available as deposit	£
Plus amount of mortgage which can be raised	£
TOTAL AMOUNT OF MONEY AVAILABLE FOR PURCHASE	£

Budget plan on completion of the transaction

Monthly budget
FOR THE PROPERTY

Mortgage repayments	£
Rates	£
Water rates	£
Gas	£
Electricity	£
Ground rent and other charges relating to leasehold property	£
Telephone	£
TV rental	£

PERSONAL

Housekeeping	£
Travelling expenses	£
Car maintenance	£
Road tax	£
Petrol	£
Clothing	£
Entertainment	£
Hire purchase	£
Savings	£
Holiday	£

INSURANCES
Mortgage protection	£
Endowment	£
Building insurance (annual)	£
Contents	£
Self and family	£
Others	£
TOTAL EXPENSES	£
MONTHLY INCOME	£

Accounting for deposits

Few agents now take deposits on resale property. Developers usually expect a deposit to be lodged, however, and any deposit held must be retained in a special clients' account for which approved insurance cover has been taken out. Make sure you issue a dated receipt for any amount taken and clearly mark it 'subject to contract and survey'.

If you hold a deposit as 'stakeholder', it must be returned in full if the sale should not proceed. You must account for any monies held on your final invoice, the amount of the deposit being deducted from the amount of commission due, unless other specific arrangements have been made through the solicitors concerned.

A deposit is treated as a goodwill gesture and an indication that the buyer intends to complete the transaction. However, it is in no way legally binding and the act of leaving a deposit with an agent is really of little significance today.

A 'holding' deposit is not the same as the deposit required on exchange of contracts. This is usually 10 per cent of purchase price and is paid by the buyer to his solicitor at the time the contract is signed and exchanged.

Conclusion

Much of the financial help and advice you are able to offer will be sought by first-time buyers or first-time sellers. The more experienced a house mover becomes, the less likely he is to need your help when it comes to sorting out mortgages or budgeting for those monthly expenses we all have to face. But as we mentioned at the beginning of this chapter, there

Your Role as Financial Adviser

are still many people who have no idea at all about the financial side of moving and maintaining a property, nor do they fully understand the different types of mortgages available to them.

You could, of course, simply direct your customer to his building society, broker or solicitor, but in doing so you immediately show your lack of concern and lack of knowledge, and that customer will probably not return to you again, or will buy from another more helpful agent. So be prepared.

Assignment 6: Understanding mortgages

Objectives
- To show knowledge of mortgage packages currently available
- To apply that knowledge to ensure that sales are negotiated only with customers who are in the best possible position to complete the transaction

Tasks
1. List four different types of mortgage package currently available.
2. List the terms and conditions under which each applies.
3. Identify the status and type of person who would benefit most from each of the mortgage packages you have listed, and give reasons.
4. From company records, identify any sales which have fallen through as a direct result of difficulties with the buyer arranging a mortgage, and list each specific reason.
5. State what action could have been taken to save the sale.
6. Prepare a list of all the reasons why a mortgage application could be turned down, and say what steps you could take in order to avoid or overcome the problems.

Assignment 7: Preparing a budget plan

Objectives
- To use your knowledge and understanding of charges and fees relating to buying and selling property in order to provide a basic budget plan for your customer
- To use budget planning to help determine the purchasing capability of your buyer

Tasks

1. Prepare a budget plan for the following applicants:

Mr Brown   A 26-year-old engineer with an annual income of £13,500. He also receives travelling and other expenses which amount to approximately £1,300 per annum. He has been employed with his present company for two years. He has a small flat to sell for £34,500 which he bought two years ago. His existing mortgage is £29,000. He wants you to sell it on a sole agency basis.

Mr Brown is hoping to buy a property with Miss Smith.

Miss Smith   A 24-year-old sales executive who has an income of £7,200 per annum plus commission currently running at approximately £120 per month. She is a first-time buyer and has been participating in the government's Homeloan Scheme and has saved £620.

2. Calculate how much money Mr Brown and Miss Smith can raise by way of a mortgage.
3. Calculate the total amount of money Mr Brown and Miss Smith will be able to afford for their new property.
4. Provide a written quotation for monthly repayments gross and net for three different types of mortgage package which may be suitable.
5. Make a complete list of all the fees they will have to pay, including a complete break-down of legal charges, and contact local solicitors and/or conveyancers to establish an estimate for these costs.
6. Provide a budget plan for Mr Brown and Miss Smith suitable for buying and selling purposes.

Chapter 5

The Final Points

Introduction

However much training you receive, there is very little that can better direct experience. As you begin your business, and it continues to grow and expand, you will learn from your experiences what to look for in a property and a buyer, and what to stay clear of or approach with caution.

So far in this book, we have discussed all the traditional methods used in selling and negotiating sales of private residential property, but each sale will differ, everyone you deal with will have their own ideas and attitudes, and all your professional contacts will have their own opinions and working methods. As you gain experience, you will learn which approach suits you and your particular working methods, and the more you are in contact with colleagues from other agencies, with surveyors, lenders and the legal profession too, you will learn who to turn to for advice and help in securing your sales.

Although estate agents are in obvious competition, they also have a great regard for each other. They know that in order to offer the best service for their clients, and secure sales for themselves, they must often work together and help each other along the way, especially when long chains of sales and purchases are involved, each one depending on the next in line until every link in the chain is complete. Only by working together and continuing to pursue a policy of professional unity can agents ensure that these chains reach a satisfactory completion.

The consumer, on the other hand, does not always appreciate exactly what the agent goes through! Once he sees a property he wants, he will do everything in his power – whatever that might be –to purchase it, and once he owns it, he will fight to the last to defend it. It is at times like these when we experience gazumping and contract races, or the same purchaser puts in offers for different properties with different agents and plays one against the other in order to get what he considers a 'bargain'. Perhaps it is this human trait from which the saying 'buying and selling property brings out the worst in people' actually stems. But whatever the reason, buying and selling property is certainly one of the most perplexing and trying experiences the consumer is ever likely to go through, and when there is a problem, or something goes drastically wrong, or someone simply changes their mind about the whole thing, who is it that gets the blame? The agent of course!

The agent is, after all, pig-in-the-middle, the go-between, in effect, between seller and buyer. Although his first responsibility is towards the client who pays his fee, he must do just as much work, sometimes even more in fact, for the buyer to make sure a successful sale is completed. The problem is that during the course of negotiations, especially when there is a chain of sales and all sorts of messages are sent along that chain, those messages get distorted or misinterpreted, especially by people who do not fully understand the intricacies of the property market. Therefore, if you are to avoid being blamed for these problems, you must make a point of being one step ahead all the time, checking and double-checking on the situation and making sure that everyone concerned does everything they should at exactly the right time. As we said in the beginning, your job does not finish as soon as you write a few letters confirming a sale.

An agency will only thrive and prosper on a good reputation, and that reputation will only be built upon negotiations which proceed smoothly to completion.

So far we have looked at the procedure for establishing sound negotiations on behalf of your clients, and discussed some of the problems which all agents experience and which can so easily damage a good reputation. Now let us look at some of the other factors which govern the world of property, bearing in mind the special position that estate agents are in, and the responsibility which rests on their shoulders.

What is a conveyance?

As an estate agent you will be referring all the legal work appertaining to your sales to your clients' solicitors or conveyancers. However, this does not mean you should not be aware of the implications of the legal processes, or what these processes are. As we have already mentioned, many sales fall through during the time the legal work is under way, and it is fair to say that in some cases, had the selling agent been aware of what was going on and why, he could well have made the appropriate moves in order to save the sale. But he can't do that unless he has some background knowledge of the steps the solicitor or conveyancer is taking.

Like the selling agent, the solicitor (or conveyancer) is working in the best interests of his client. This could be the seller or the buyer, but the same solicitor cannot work for both, although two separate members of the same company could be involved, one representing the seller and the other the buyer.

The Final Points

So let us now look at what the solicitor does after he has received your letter of confirmation that a sale has been agreed.

The seller's solicitor will draw up a draft contract and send it to the buyer's solicitor. This draft will include the price of the property, a description of the property, the buyer's and the seller's names, whether the property is leasehold or freehold, and if there are any restrictions on the use of the property.

The aim of the buyer's solicitor is then quite simple: to make sure the seller is legally entitled to sell the property in the first place, and to ensure that there is nothing about the property, its land or its surroundings which might either now or in the future restrict the new owner from living happily in the property.

In order to establish proof of ownership, the solicitor will need to inspect the Land Registry if the property is already registered. This will provide all the information he needs relating to the owner, and previous owners, of the property. If the property is not registered, his task is more difficult because he will then have to check the deeds in order to establish a 'good root'. This means checking the details of the property going back at least 15 years. If the property is new, then the solicitor will check the transactions on the land itself.

A *conveyance* is the document transferring ownership from seller to buyer if the property has an unregistered title, and a *transfer* is the document transferring ownership from seller to buyer if the property has a registered title.

The buyer's solicitor also carries out various enquiries and searches. Local searches are made through the local authority and a standard printed form can be used for this purpose. Such searches will reveal some of the information the solicitor needs, but other questions relating to the property will be sent direct to the seller and/or his solicitor. Here, again, a form setting out standard questions can be used.

The areas covered during these 'preliminary enquiries' include:

- if there is valid planning permission appertaining to the property
- shared rights of access such as shared driveways or forecourts
- details of other 'easements' such as rights of way across the property, if services such as drainage cross the property and, if so, the responsibilities and rights associated with them
- the liabilities concerning the maintenance of boundary walls and fences, and the exact positioning of boundaries
- any proposed development of the surrounding area
- whether a compulsory purchase order is likely to be imposed
- what duties and responsibilities fall upon the owner
- details of any 'restrictive convenants' which may apply, eg no

- caravans to be parked on the premises, the premises may not be used as a business
- details of any guarantees applicable to the property such as a guarantee for timber treatment
- confirmation of items included in the sale and/or to be sold by separate arrangement
- details of any money which could be claimed by the local authority, eg the local authority may plan to take over the private road fronting the property and the owner may be asked to contribute towards this expense
- if the property is leasehold, the terms and conditions of the lease must be checked and approved.

At present, local authorities tend to take a considerable time to reply to local searches received from solicitors and this often causes delays. It has been suggested that local authorities should be required by law to reply within a set period of time, or that all the information is computerised to expedite the whole procedure. However, until then the old method must be used and solicitors cannot be held responsible for any delays caused by non-receipt of replies to enquiries.

The draft contract could be passed from solicitor to solicitor several times before the final wording is approved and accepted by both parties. The final document will include the following information:

- full name of the seller and the buyer
- occupation of the seller and the buyer
- the capacity in which the seller sells, ie owner, trustee or other
- address and description of the property
- leasehold or freehold (if leasehold, details of the lease, including period of the lease and ground rent payable)
- the deposit (usually 10 per cent of purchase price) payable on exchange of contracts
- the completion date if known at this stage
- the title number of the property if it is registered with the Land Registry
- use of the property, ie dwelling house, business premises
- details of any restrictive or other convenants
- any other conditions, agreements or declarations
- any special conditions which might apply
- if the property is to be sold with vacant possession on completion
- interest on any unpaid purchase money or delayed completion
- inventory of items to be purchased separately together with price.

The Final Points

The buyer should raise any queries with his solicitor, and ask him to verify any matters which are not clear, or which the buyer does not fully understand, especially when they relate to his responsibilities and obligations once he takes occupation.

Where a property is purchased jointly, two kinds of ownership can apply. *A joint tenancy* is an arrangement under which neither party can sell without the other's agreement, and if one party should die, the other will automatically inherit the share. This is the most common form of co-ownership chosen by husband and wife.

A tenancy in common is slightly different. Here each owner may dispose of his share of the property as he wishes. This can be during the lifetime of the owner or by will.

Once all the enquiries have been answered, confirmation of the mortgage arrangements have been received and the draft contract approved, the buyer signs the contract and pays the required deposit and the seller signs the contract and accepts the deposit. Contracts are then exchanged.

It is not a good idea for a contract to be signed by either party unless their solicitor has gone through the documentation step by step with them personally, and explained what all the legal jargon in which such documents are invariably couched actually means. Unfortunately, there are still some solicitors who are happy to send this important paperwork through the post with a note asking their clients to sign where indicated and ring if there is a query. If by any chance someone brings a contract to you for an explanation, send him straight to his solicitor or conveyancer.

Until exchange has taken place, no legal commitment to complete the transaction has been made, and either party can withdraw from the deal at any time, but as soon as contracts are exchanged, the matter becomes legally binding on both parties.

If the buyer fails to complete the purchase after contracts have been exchanged, he will lose his deposit. If the seller's loss is more than that amount, he can sue for the balance. If the seller fails to complete the purchase after contracts have been exchanged, the buyer can instruct a court to order him to do so and to compensate him for any loss he has incurred.

As soon as the contracts are exchanged, the buyer is legally responsible for insuring the property. The lender's solicitor provides the mortgage deeds and forwards them to the buyer's solicitor. These must be checked and signed in order to ensure that the mortgage money will be available for completion. If the property is registered, the transfer deed must be approved (or conveyance if land is not registered) and signed.

The seller's solicitor will draw up a completion statement which sets out exactly how much must be paid on completion and this is forwarded to the buyer's solicitor. On completion the buyer's solicitor hands over the money owed in exchange for the deeds and the keys of the property. The seller must then pay his solicitor's fee, including your fee as the selling agent, and the solicitor will forward this amount to you.

The deeds are handed to the building society, as they are the security for the mortgage. The title deed is sent to the Land Registry for a new entry to be made.

If you hold the key to a property, or have arranged to take possession of the key from the seller on the day of completion, you must not hand the key to the buyer until you have contacted the seller's solicitor and had confirmation that legal completion has taken place and the money has been received. This may mean that the buyer has to wait around, complete with removal van, for some time before he can gain access. Don't forget that a signature must be obtained for the key when it is passed to the new owner.

The seller should leave in the property everything which has previously been agreed and/or shown on your specification. If there are items included on your specification which are not left in the property and cannot be retrieved from the seller, then you could be held responsible for these items. Such is the importance of making sure your specification is carefully formulated and signed approval of it is received from the seller, right at the beginning of the negotiations.

Although the aims of the solicitor seem fairly straightforward, achieving the required result is not at all as simple as it may appear, even when backed by a series of pre-printed forms and guide-line documentation, and there are a number of points at which problems do occur and sales start to totter. For example:

- difficulties with mortgage arrangements and/or surveys (as previously mentioned)
- problems arising from local searches where new roads or local developments may affect the property
- restrictive convenants where the buyer may not be able to keep a horse or other livestock in the garden
- where the terms of a lease prove to be far too much of a liability for the new owner to undertake
- where the new owner is committed to some financial outlay.

These are just a few examples of the difficulties which could be encountered and which could possibly persuade the buyer to withdraw from the deal. The seller too could change his mind and withdraw, but if you have been monitoring the progress of the sale as you should, then you will be aware of the difficulties and can take the necessary action to save the sale. This could mean renegotiating a lower purchase price, or making some reduction in your commission. But where it is obvious that the buyer has no intention of completing the transaction and decides to withdraw, you must make sure you have already lined up another buyer ready to step in and take over.

If you haven't, then no doubt another agent with the same property on his register will have. Where a chain of sales and purchases is involved, then the old problem of a 'collapse' once more rears its ugly head. Unless you can move swiftly on behalf of the seller, then with the collapse goes part of your good reputation – even though you may have had no control over the matter whatsoever.

Being aware of the legal processes, however, gives you a much more in-depth appreciation of the exact position of your sale at any one time. This in itself allows you to keep abreast of the situation and pass on all the right information to the right people, and take all the right steps at exactly the right time in order to ensure that completion is reached to the satisfaction of everyone involved.

National Association of Estate Agents

The National Association of Estate Agents was established in 1962, although a loose association was formed some considerable time before that. The Association represents the interests of those practising as selling agents, and aims continually to assess and improve standards of professionalism within the field. It constantly monitors legislation with regard to every aspect of the sale of property and land, and offers advice and new ideas to its members in order to ensure that they provide the best possible service for the consumer.

Codes of conduct set by the Association are high and many of its members are bonded members, which means that consumers are protected against any loss of deposit monies, and can contact the Association if they feel the agent is not conducting his business properly.

As a selling agent you are not bound to become a member of any association, but membership does offer proof to consumers that you carry out your business to a high standard and, as a bonded member, that any deposit they leave with you will be protected. Details of membership can be obtained through the Association.

Members of the Association meet at regular intervals to discuss matters relating to selling and current market trends. As the market is in a continual state of change, these meetings provide an opportunity for agents to discuss strategies and put forward new ideas within their own particular area.

Association members also run the *National Homelink Service*. People moving to new areas across the country can contact their nearest Association member who will be able to locate an agent from the area and arrange for particulars of properties on that agent's register to be forwarded to the customer.

More than 500 agents now offer this service nationwide, and each is provided with a national directory of agents participating in the scheme; although no guarantees can be made that a suitable property is readily available, it is yet another way in which agents can work together to provide the best possible service for their customers.

Further professional qualifications

As your business begins to grow you will find it necessary to extend your selling skills further, or to enlist the help of surveyors and other professionally qualified people in order to meet the demands made by your customers.

Many agents are professionally qualified surveyors and members of the Royal Institution of Chartered Surveyors (RICS) or the Incorporated Society of Valuers and Auctioneers (ISVA) and combine house and land selling with many other services related to the profession. These include:

- carrying out RICS House and Flat Buyer's Report and Valuation
- valuations for the purposes of assessing the open market value of land and/or property
- rental valuations for the purposes of rent reviews
- preparation of fair rent applications
- valuation for probate
- valuation of goods and chattels for insurance
- valuation for rating purposes
- valuation for compulsory purchase
- dealing with insurance claims in respect of house building insurance
- valuation for capital gains tax
- structural surveys
- providing advice for grant applications
- providing advice for refurbishment of listed buildings
- providing planning and building services which cover legislation appertaining to town and country planning
- undertaking planning appeals on behalf of clients
- measurement surveys of land and buildings and preparation of plans
- property management, including commercial and retail premises
- lettings.

Ongoing training in any profession is essential in today's business world. Not only does it provide contact with other people within a particular field, but also the opportunity for students continually to improve and update their working methods, incorporating modern techniques and new technology. It also stimulates new ideas and new concepts, and must not be overlooked, especially by someone starting in business for the very first time. Failure to make the effort – and it is an effort to take on extra studies when you are working full time – results in your company dropping behind and losing customers. So let us look in more detail at some of the professional qualifications relating to property and land sales, and what you have to do to achieve them.

The Incorporated Society of Valuers and Auctioneers (ISVA)

Being one of the principal professional organisations in the estate profession, the ISVA have external examinations which are administered by independent examination bodies.

The aims of the Society are to ensure that their members provide a professionally and technically competent service, and members must abide by the code of professional conduct expected of them. The Society also strive to maintain and continually improve the status of their members.

A corporate member of the ISVA is recognised as a fully qualified valuer and can progress to senior level; valuation skills can be extended to cover specialist areas such as fine arts and chattels.

You must become a student member of the Society on enrolment for their courses, and these are usually run by technical colleges and colleges of higher education from whom full details can be obtained.

The examinations can be taken in a series of three stages or, alternatively, Graduate Preliminary, Graduate Final or Direct Final examination. All candidates must be student members of the Society to be eligible. Candidates are also required to meet standards applicable to the Society's professional assessment if they wish to be elected to corporate membership during a period of practical experience.

Entry qualifications vary and are set out in detail on the prospectus provided, but special consideration is given to applications from members who are over 24 years of age with professional experience.

The three-year course covers the following areas:

valuation
land use and planning
economics
building construction
taxation
land law

landlord and tenant law
land and property economics
business management
statutory valuations
development law
property development
property management
agency practice
tutorial and project work.

The above applies to the general practice division.

There are other divisions too, such as Fine Arts and Chattels and Graduate courses. To find out more contact the ISVA direct and/or your local teaching body.

The Royal Institution of Chartered Surveyors (RICS)

The Institute was founded in 1868 and incorporated by Royal Charter in 1881, and its aims are to advance and facilitate the acquisition of knowledge within the profession of the surveyor.

Candidates must become student members of the RICS to participate in their courses and examination enquiries, applications, Candidates' Guide to the Examinations and Rules and Syllabus may be obtained from the Education and Membership Department, Royal Institution of Chartered Surveyors, Norden House, Basing View, Basingstoke RG21 2HN.

Here again, courses are run by colleges, higher education institutes and polytechnics from whom a complete prospectus can be obtained.

The College of Estate Management

The College was founded by 1919 and incorporated by Royal Charter in 1922. Her Majesty the Queen is patron. The College runs the CEM Certificate in Residential Estate Agency which is designed specifically for residential negotiators.

It is a correspondence course incorporating a compulsory three-day residential course, and culminating in a five-paper examination. A certificate is awarded to students which outlines the student's achievements, and it is possible to be awarded a certificate with distinction.

Full details of courses and entry fees together with application forms can be obtained from the College of Estate Management, Whiteknights, Reading RG6 2AW.

The syllabus covers the following areas in detail:

estate agency practice
– sales practice

– marketing
– management
law and the estate agent
– agency
– property
domestic building construction
valuation of residential property
residential course.

Other courses
There are many other courses on offer; for example, from the Institute of Housing but there are other related studies, and most can be taken full time, part time or by correspondence. If you are interested, you should contact your nearest teaching body to obtain details of entry criteria, course content, dates, fees and all relevant information.

Despite the advantages offered by professional qualifications and training programmes, it must be said that there are still some professionally qualified selling agents who do not provide the sort of service expected. Sadly, too, companies with offices nationwide sometimes lose the 'personal touch' that only the smaller, more intimate agencies are able to offer. So don't be put off by competition from these groups. There is still room for the small business which is able to keep in touch with customers and clients on a personal basis, and show concern and attention to aspects of house buying and selling that larger companies are often too busy to have time for.

Remember that most people dread buying and selling property because of the difficulties and complications associated with it. But the friendly 'shop on the corner' can often provide that special something which makes it all much easier for them, even if it is just somewhere to come and chat over the problems in the knowledge that advice and help will be offered wherever possible. An attentive manner, a cup of coffee and a quiet chat are sometimes all that are needed to pave the way towards a successful sale, or to the receipt of an instruction to sell.

Success breeds growth
As your business begins to prosper you will find yourself dealing more and more with administrative and managerial matters and with less time for measuring up property and taking prospective buyers to view. You will want to expand the company, improve and update your existing premises, take on more staff to branch out into business transfer and

auctioneering, and perhaps open another office in an adjoining territory for which additional working capital may well be needed.

If you have been working as a sole trader, you may at this point feel it necessary to work more closely with a professionally qualified surveyor and you could raise more capital by taking on a surveyor as a working partner. However, you and your partner will still be personally responsible for any debts the business might incur if it should subsequently fail.

The alternative solution could be to form a limited company so that you can sell shares in the business to raise some of the additional capital you need. If you do well, your shareholders will receive a share of the profits, called a dividend, and the money raised from the sale – your share capital – will provide more collateral and offer a more substantial base on which to borrow additional funds from the bank if you need them. Much will depend on the size of your company, turnover, balance sheet and number of employees – it is not quite as easy as it sounds, especially for the small private limited company – so you will need the help and advice of your accountant and solicitor to set it up properly, and to explain the salient points of the Companies Acts, the most important being that if the company fails, liability is limited to the owners' investment, and their personal wealth cannot be touched.

If your business growth is such that this stage is reached, and a company is formed, you will need to draw up and fully understand the Memorandum of Association and the Articles of Association as in Table A of the Companies Act 1948 which, as we mentioned earlier in the book, set out exactly what the company is entitled to do and the rules under which it is to be run. Also shown is the way in which shares can be bought and sold.

There are certainly many decisions to make at this time, decisions which must not be made lightly and without professional advice, so talk to your accountant and your solicitor before you do anything at all.

If you are thinking of opening another office, it is wise to consider a location which will complement your existing position. The number of properties for sale in any given area varies a great deal and often an agent may see his own area as being slow with little for sale, while on its borders turnover is greater. Instructions to sell those properties, however, are given to agents within the 'sales circle' and it is in a situation such as this that the agent with offices in both areas will benefit. As you can see, branching out and expanding your business to neighbouring areas has its advantages, so if you are ready to make the move, choose your new area with care. Research it thoroughly and check competition just as you did in the beginning, although now you will have your own good name and reputation to help you along the way.

Selling property in Scotland

In Scotland, the legal system regarding property is different. Efforts have been made to encourage a change in England towards some of the Scottish methods to make the English approach a little more straightforward. However, we are still a long way from a time when buying and selling property becomes as easy as buying and selling a garden shed. In years to come, estate agents, and everyone else involved in the process, will be able to offer a more satisfactory way of ensuring that the completion of transactions is reached quickly and efficiently. Until then it must rest with every selling agent to do all in his power to make this complicated business run as smoothly as possible for customers.

In Scotland the majority of sales are carried out by the solicitors acting on behalf of the seller, and solicitors have their own property centres where particulars of properties can be obtained.

At present there are only a few estate agents in Scotland, although the numbers are beginning to grow, and they operate in much the same way as their English counterparts.

From the property centre, the customer can obtain particulars of the properties for sale, together with the name of the owner, the solicitor handling the transaction, the minimum price required, rateable value and details of the property itself.

Arrangements to view are made through the solicitor, and the buyer can discuss with the seller the price, the date of entry and the details of any contents which may be purchased with the sale. If the buyer is still interested at this point, he contacts his solicitor who in turn contacts the seller's solicitor and the buyer's interest is formally noted. The seller's solicitor or estate agent can then undertake not to sell the house to anyone else unless the interested party is first contacted and invited to put forward an offer.

The buyer must then arrange a suitable loan from a building society, and the next most important step is to arrange a survey. It is upon the surveyor's report that the final figure put forward as an offer should be based, and if several people have had surveys carried out there will be a great deal of competition, pushing up the price accordingly. Here, offers made in respect of the items to be left in the property, or the date of entry, can be deciding factors when the seller has to choose which offer to accept.

Where a number of people are interested in the property the seller's solicitor will fix a closing date by which all offers must be made and the seller and his solicitor will then go through the offers on that date to decide which one to accept.

The solicitors will then negotiate the terms of the contract by letter, which takes just a couple of days, and a final letter is then drafted and sent. At this point the matter becomes legally binding and is the equivalent of the exchange of contracts in England.

The contract is called missives in Scotland, and once this stage is concluded it is only a matter of weeks before completion – called settlement – is reached.

The conveyance itself is not unlike that in England, but as you can see, by accepting an offer the deal becomes binding at that stage, whereas in England either party can withdraw right up until the time contracts are exchanged. The problems experienced with chains and gazumping in England are therefore far less likely to be experienced by buyers and sellers in Scotland.

Lettings

Many agents now act as representatives for owners wishing to rent out their properties, and this provides additional income for the agent, although it should not be undertaken unless you have a good working knowledge of the law regarding landlord and tenant and the Rent Acts. If you are in any doubt, consult your solicitor in order to make sure you undertake the work correctly and follow the necessary procedures properly.

Agents' charges are based on monthly rents received and are a percentage of that rent, perhaps 10 or 15 per cent depending upon their agreement with the owner. A charge is also made for drawing up the relevant documents each time a new occupier takes up the rental, and it is the new occupier who will pay for this.

An inventory of the contents of the property must be prepared initially, and each time a person moves in he must tick off and sign that the inventory is accurate and nothing is missing. When that same person moves out, the agent must check the inventory again and if any items are damaged or missing (not due to normal wear and tear), an appropriate charge must be made. This amount can be deducted from the deposit paid by the occupier when he signed the documents before moving in.

One month's rental is usually paid in advance, together with an appropriate deposit. This can be the equivalent of another month's rental, which is returnable at the time the property is vacated, less any deductions for damage.

The agent must make sure that the person taking up the lease is reliable and, therefore, before any agreements are signed or keys handed over, you must take up a personal reference, a professional reference which could be from a solicitor, accountant or doctor, a bank and an employment reference. Only if these are satisfactory should the documentation be signed.

It is a wise precaution to draw up the terms and conditions of leases in conjunction with your solicitor and, of course, these must be approved by the owner. He may prefer no children or pets, for instance, and this must be taken into account together with the term of notice required by either party.

Glossary of legal terms

Legal jargon is almost as confusing as estate agent's jargon, so the following glossary has been provided to shed some light on it:

absolute title true and unquestionable ownership of property
abstract of title a summary of the relevant documents providing proof of ownership
advance the loan or capital sum
annuity mortgage repayment mortgage
assignment ownership of property or insurance policy transferred to another
assignment of lease document transferring ownership of a lease from one person to another
banker's draft a cheque issued by a bank instead of cash
bridging loan short-term loan (usually from a bank) used by purchaser as deposit on exchange of contracts, or to complete a purchase while he waits for the sale of his home
charge certificate document issued by the Land Registry on a registered property and held by the mortgagee
collateral property pledged as a guarantee against money borrowed
completion point where transaction is completed and money is exchanged for the title deeds and keys to the property
completion statement final account provided by the seller's solicitor setting out the amount payable by the buyer on completion; price, apportionment of rates, and deposits will be taken into account
contract written agreement between buyer and seller which, when signed, binds both parties to the agreement
convertible term policy policy which allows a borrower to change from a term policy to another type, eg an endowment policy
conveyance document transferring ownership of property and/or land with unregistered title from seller to buyer
conveyancing common term for the legal work undertaken when buying and selling property
decreasing term insurance life insurance where the amount of cover decreases throughout the term of the policy, eg mortgage protection policy

decreasing term policy policy which allows for the sum insured to be decreased as the term of the money advanced continues, but leaves enough money to pay off the outstanding loan

discharge of registered charge form showing repayment of mortgage on registered property

draft contract suggested wording which must be agreed before the final contract is drawn up

draft transfer suggested wording for the transfer document

early redemption repayment of mortgage before the end of the term

easements rights of way across a property or its land

endowment insurance life insurance which will pay out a lump sum in the event of the death of the insured, or on a specified date

endowment mortgage a loan which remains outstanding throughout the specified term and on which only interest is paid

equity net value of a property after the mortgage has been deducted

fee simple absolute ownership of property and land (freehold)

filed plan the way in which registered property is identified at the Land Registry Office

freehold absolute ownership of property and land

good root evidence proving ownership of property such as mortgage deed

ground rent annual rent for a lease

initial year the period between the granting of a mortgage and the beginning of the lender's next financial year

joint tenants more than one person co-owning a property; when one dies, his share of the property passes to his survivor(s)

land certificate certificate provided by the Land Registry showing details of the land registered with them

land registry fee payment made by buyer to register ownership of property or land at the Land Registry; the scale of fees is set by the government

leasehold land and/or property held under lease for which a rental is paid for a fixed number of years

legal charge mortgage deed

lessor one who grants a lease

level term policy policy which provides a fixed amount of cover for the full period of the advanced sum of money

lien legal right of a person to hold the property of another as security in respect of a loan

mortgage loan made for property purchase and for which the property itself offers security for the loan

mortgagee lender

mortgage indemnity policy compulsory additional insurance required by lender when loan exceeds the normal percentage of valuation of the property; also known as a mortgage guarantee policy

mortgagor borrower

positive covenant certain deed and/or activity which must be carried out by the owner on or to his property and land

possessory title ownership of land by someone who may have a better right than the registered owner

preliminary enquiries questions the buyer's solicitor asks about the property and its land before the final contract can be completed and signed

principal the amount of loan on which interest is calculated

purchaser one who buys a property or land

redemption paying off an existing loan

registered land land with title registered at HM Land Registry with legal ownership guaranteed

repayment mortgage loan where part of the capital and the interest is paid back throughout the term of the loan

restrictive covenant certain deed and/or activity which must not be carried out by the owner on or to his property and land

specific performance the successful completion of a transaction

stamp duty a tax on legal documents

subject to contract the stage during which either party can withdraw from the transaction without incurring penalties

tenancy in common two or more people co-owning a property where one can dispose of his share as he chooses; it does not automatically pass to the other owner

tenure whether a property is freehold or leasehold

term of mortgage number of years over which the loan extends

title deeds documents showing ownership of property and land

transfer document transferring ownership of registered property from seller to buyer

under offer when a seller has received an offer for his property, but the transaction is not complete

vacant possession property is left empty and unoccupied when seller moves out

vacating receipt endorsement of mortgage deed showing that a mortgage on unregistered property has been repaid

vendor person, usually the owner, selling the property

Conclusion

There are many factors which influence the buying and selling of property, and many factors which influence the way different professions carry out their role within the field. But each is part of the whole, and if successful sales are to be forthcoming, none must try to work alone.

The businessman setting out as an estate agent for the very first time should make an effort to introduce himself to other professional people in his area with whom he will undoubtedly be in contact during his negotiations. The saying 'it is who you know rather than what you know that is important' is to some extent true. In the early days of your business activities you will want to be recommended by people – who better than those with whom you will be dealing anyway!

Assignment 8: Final project

Provide at least *four* case studies of sales you have negotiated.

Objectives
Case studies must provide evidence of your competence and show that you know and apply your skills to provide a fully comprehensive service for all your customers, which ensures that all enquiries received are negotiated so that completed sales are forthcoming.

Criteria for achievement
Case studies must demonstrate your *personal* involvement in the following areas:

- initial client contact
- valuation of property
- escorted viewing
- negotiating the sale
- advising customers on aspects of mortgages and/or arranging the mortgage
- problem solving
- the provision of additional services for your client, such as surveys or other technical advice
- evidence that appropriate follow-up techniques were applied
- evidence that your knowledge of the legal aspect of the negotiations was used effectively.

Notes to trainers
The assignments in this book have been designed to give trainees an opportunity to use their knowledge and skills effectively in each area of estate agency covered in the preceding chapter.

The Final Points

Trainers should check all written work to ensure that each objective has been reached and that trainees have not overlooked any important feature. Trainees should be able to apply a self-critique to their work in conjunction with your own assessment of achievement.

The following profile can be completed throughout the training programme and will assist trainers in assessing the standards reached by the trainee.

Objective	*How Demonstrated*	*Date*
1. Demonstrate ability to identify the needs of individual customers quickly and efficiently		
2. Demonstrate ability to communicate effectively with customers at all levels		
3. Identify potential buyers		
4. Identify potential sellers		
5. Provide evidence that efficient viewing arrangements are made and adequate follow-up procedures undertaken		
6. Provide evidence that ongoing communication with all applicants is maintained		

Objective	How Demonstrated	Date
7. Provide evidence that all hand-outs are properly presented and information contained therein is accurate and in no way misleading		
8. Provide evidence that trainee can deal effectively with all enquiries and show a high ratio of sales to enquiries		
9. Demonstrate effective negotiating skills		
10. Provide evidence that trainee can deal effectively with gazumping and understands its implications		
11. Demonstrate in-depth knowledge of trainee's territory		
12. Provide evidence of criteria on which valuations are made		
13. Identify valuation techniques detrimental to the profession		

Objective	How Demonstrated	Date
14. Provide evidence of a successful valuation from which a sale has been made		
15. Understand the different types of mortgage advances available		
15.1 Demonstrate knowledge of how each mortgage package is applied		
15.2 Demonstrate ability to offer sound financial advice to customers		
16. Demonstrate knowledge of restrictions which apply to advances and why they apply		
16.1 Provide evidence that this knowledge is used to advise and assist both buyers and sellers		
17. Demonstrate ability to identify areas where trainee's personal performance could be improved		
18. Demonstrate ability to integrate trainee's role with other members of staff to ensure that customers always receive a first-class service		

Objective	How Demonstrated	Date
19. Provide evidence of understanding insurances including: (a) contents (b) rebuilding (c) mortgage protection (d) endowment		
20. Demonstrate understanding of legal terms		
21. Provide evidence of satisfactory understanding of conveyancing and related legal work in order to advise customers as and when necessary		
22. Provide evidence that trainee uses his skills and knowledge to help and advise all customers, thus benefitting both himself and his company by providing a first-class service at all times		

Appendix

Sources of Further Information

Alliance of Small Firms and Self-Employed People
42 Vine Road
East Molesey
Surrey KT8 9LF
01–979 2293

Architects' Registration Council
73 Hallam Street
London W1N 6EE
01–580 5861

British Association of Removers
279 Gray's Inn Road
London WC1X 8SY
01–837 3088

British Franchise Association
Franchise Chambers
75a Bell Street
Henley on Thames
Oxfordshire RG9 2BD
0491 578049

British Insurance Association
Aldermary House
Queen Street
London EC4N 1TU
01–248 4477

British Insurance Brokers' Association
BIBA House
14 Bevis Marks
London EC3N 7AT
01–623 9043

133

British Wood Preserving Association
150 Southampton Row
London WC1B 5AL
01-837 8217

Building Societies Association
3 Savile Row
London W1X 1AF
01-437 0655

Chartered Association of Certified Accountants
29 Lincoln's Inn Fields
London WC2A 3EE
01-242 6855

College of Estate Management
Whiteknights
Reading RG6 2AW
0734 861101

Companies Registration Office
Companies House
55 City Road
London EC1Y 1BB
01-253 9393

Corporation of Finance Brokers
13 Ashleigh Road
Yatton
Bristol BS19 4DE
0934 835008

Corporation of Mortgage Brokers
PO Box 101
Guildford
Surrey GU1 2HZ
0438 39121

Council of Licensed Conveyancers
Golden Cross House
9 Duncannon Street
London EC2N 4JF
01-210 4603

Appendix

Country Landowners' Association
16 Belgrave Square
London SW1X 8PQ
01-235 0511

Finance Houses Association
18 Upper Grosvenor Street
London W1X 9PB
01-491 2783

Financial Intermediaries', Managers' and Brokers' Regulators Association
22 Great Tower Street
London EC3R 5AQ
01-283 4814

House Building Advisory Bureau
353 Strand
London WC2R 0HU
01-836 5263

Incorporated Association of Architects and Surveyors
Jubilee House
Billing Brook Road
Weston Favell
Northampton NN3 4NW
0604 404121

Incorporated Society of Valuers and Auctioneers
3 Cadogan Gate
London SW1X 0AS
01-235 2282

Institute of Chartered Accountants in England and Wales
Chartered Accountants' Hall
1 Moorgate Place
London EC2P 2BJ
01-628 7060

Institute of Housing
9 White Lion Street
London N1 9XJ
01-837 4280

Insurance Brokers' Registration Council
15 St Helen's Place
London EC3A 6DS
01-588 4387

HM Land Registry
32 Lincoln's Inn Fields
London WC2A 3PH
01-405 3488

Law Society
113 Chancery Lane
London WC2A 1PL
01-242 1222

Law Society of Scotland
PO Box 75
26 Drumsheugh Gardens
Edinburgh EH3 7YR
031-226 7411

National Association of Conveyancers
44 London Road
Kingston upon Thames
Surrey KT2 6QF
01-549 3636

National Association of Estate Agents
Arbon House
21 Jury Street
Warwick CV34 4EH
0926 496800

National Association of Homeowners
PO Box 1122
FREEPOST
Shrewsbury
Shropshire SY3 7BR
0743 67541

National Federation of Self-Employed and Small Businesses
32 St Anne's Road West
Lytham St Anne's
Lancashire FY8 1NY
0253 720911

National Home Improvement Council
26 Store Street
London WC1E 7BT
01–636 2562

National House Building Council
58 Portland Place
London W1N 4BU
01–637 1248

National Institute of Conveyancing Agents
41A Prospect Hil
Swindon SN1 2JS
0793 692570

Registrar of Companies
Companies House
Crown Way
Maindy
Cardiff CF4 2UZ
0222 388588

Royal Institution of Chartered Surveyors
12 Great George Street
Parliament Square
London SW1P 3AD
01–222 7000

Royal Town Planning Institute
26 Portland Place
London W0N 4BE
01–636 9107

Small Firms Centres:
You can contact your nearest centre by dialling 100 and asking for Freefone Enterprise.

Other help and advice for the small business is provided through local Jobcentres.

Note: Copies of the Acts mentioned in this book can be obtained from any booksellers who are agents for HMSO or direct from HMSO Stationery Suppliers, or law stationers. The National Association of Estate Agents have produced a guide to the Estate Agents Act 1979 and this can be obtained direct from the Association for a small fee.

Further Reading from Kogan Page

Be Your Own Company Secretary, A J Scrine, 1987
Business Rip-Offs and How to Avoid Them, Tony Attwood, 1987
Buying and Renovating Houses for Profit, 2nd edition, K Ludman and R B Buchanan, 1988
Choosing and Using Professional Advisers, editor Paul Chaplin, 1986
Customer Service, Malcolm Peel, 1987
Financial Management for the Small Business: The Daily Telegraph Guide, 2nd edition, Colin Barrow, 1988
Getting Started: How to Set Up Your Own Business, Robson Rhodes, 1988
How to Buy a Business: The Daily Telegraph Guide, Peter Farrell, 1983
How to Choose Business Premises: A Guide for the Small Firm, Howard Green, Brian Chalkley and Paul Foley, 1986
Law for the Small Business: The Daily Telegraph Guide, 5th edition, Patricia Clayton, 1987
Working for Yourself: The Daily Telegraph Guide to Self-Employment, 10th edition, Godfrey Golzen, 1988

Index

Advertising 29, 61
Arrangement fee 104
Articles of Association 10, 122
Auctions 67–8

Bank loan 12
Boards 31
Bookkeeping 25–7
Bridging finance 50, 105
British Association of
  Removers 104, 133
British Insurance Association 94, 133
British Insurance Brokers' Association 19, 133
Brokers 19, 20
Budgets 105–8
Building society agency 18
Building up a register 61–81
Business image 27–32
Business names 27
Business plan 12
Business premises 15
Buyers' market 75

Card index 35
Chains 43, 49
Chartered Association of
  Certified Accountants 26, 134
College of Estate Management
  120, 134
Companies Act 10, 27, 122
Completion 55, 115
Computer systems 16
Contract of employment 22–4
Contract races 51, 57
Consumer Credit Act 1974 19

Conveyancing 102, 105, 112–17
Corporation of Mortgage
  Brokers 19, 134
Council houses 79–80
Council of Licensed Conveyancers 102, 134

Day books 34
Deposits 55, 108
Down-valuations 57
Draft contract 113

Easements 113
Employees 20–24
Enterprise Allowance 14
Estate Agents Act 1979 32, 55, 74
Estate agents' fees 25, 78, 104
Exchanging contracts 50, 115
Executors 78

File notes 34
Financial advice, giving 82–110
Financial Intermediaries',
  Managers' and Brokers'
  Regulatory Association
  (FIMBRA) 19, 135
Financial Services Act 19
First-time buyer 49
Fixtures and fittings 54, 72, 103
Flat Buyer's Report and
  Valuation 20, 96
For Sale boards 31
Full planning consent 17

Gazumping 56
Glossary 125

Health and Safety at Work Act 1974 17
Home improvement grants 66
Homeloan Scheme 85
House Buyer's Report and Valuation 20, 96
House Rebuilding Cost Index 93
Housing Act 1980 77, 79
Housing and Building Control Act 79

Incorporated Society of Valuers and Auctioneers 20, 68, 118, 119, 135
Inland Revenue 21
Inspection fees 58, 95, 99, 100
Institute of Chartered Accountants 26, 135
Insurance:
   convertible term 93
   decreasing term 93
   endowment 94
   guarantee 92
   household 94
   house rebuilding 93
   level term 93
   mortgage protection 86, 92
Insurance Brokers' Registration Council 19, 136
Interest 87, 91

Job description 22
Joint tenancy 115

Keys 47, 116

Land Registration Acts 103
Land Registry 103, 136
Land Transfer Acts 103
Law Society 68, 102, 136
Leasehold Reform Act 1967 76
Leases 67, 76, 77
Legal expenses 102
Lenders:
   banks 89
   employers 89
   local authority 88
   private 89
Letters of confirmation 52, 53, 54
Lettings 124
Limited company 10
Listed buildings 64

Mailing list record 42
Mailing systems 36
Maternity pay 22
Measuring up 71
Memorandum of Association 10, 122
MIRAS (mortgage interest relief at source) 90
Missives 124
Mortgage:
   annuity 85
   capital repayment 85
   constraints 66, 91
   endowment 86, 94
   guaranteed 88
   in principle 49, 84
   interest 85, 87
   low cost 86
   low start 88
   non profit 86
   offer 101
   pension 87
   redemption 103
   term of 91
   with profit 86
Mortgage application forms 99
Mortgagee 103
Multiple agency 69
Multiples of salary 83

National Association of Conveyancers 102, 136
National Association of Estate Agents 32, 55, 63, 117, 136
National Homelink Service 117

Index

National House Building Council 78, 137
National Institute of Conveyancing Agents 102, 137
National Insurance contributions 9, 10, 21

Offers 51
Office equipment 13
On-site sales 77–8
Overdraft 12

Part exchange 77
Partnership Act 1890 11
Partnership agreement 11
Part possession 79
PAYE 10, 21
Personal planning consent 17
Photographs 45
Preliminary enquiries 113
Premises 15–17
Private loans 14
Product knowledge 45
Professional qualifications 118–19

Record keeping 33–7
Redemption charge 103
Redundancy 24
Registrar of Companies 10, 26, 137
Removal costs 104
Rent Act 79, 124
Restrictive covenants 113
Retentions 57, 58
Royal Institution of Chartered Surveyors 20, 63, 93, 96, 118, 119, 137

Sales record book 37
Scotland, selling property in 123–4
Searches 104, 113
Sellers' market 76
Settlement 124
Sick pay 21
Sitting tenants 79
Small Firms Centres 138
Sole agency 62, 69
Sole selling rights 69
Sole trader 9
Specifications 70–75
Stamp duty 103
Starting up 9–40
Statutory insurance 18
Structural survey 20, 97
Sub agency 69
Subject to contract 52

Tax 21; see also PAYE *and* Value added tax
Tax relief 87, 90
Temporary planning consent 17
Tenancy in common 115
Touting 63
Trade Descriptions Act 74
Transfer 113

Under offer 52
Unfair dismissal 24

Valuations 63, 75
Value added tax 9, 24, 104
Viewing appointments 35, 46–8

Window displays 15, 28

Youth Training Scheme 21